Skating was my m  the world revolved a anything else from the age of eleven to now, and I'm still in that dream, or computer simulation, or whatever it is. When I try to relive and remember the time when skateboarding sucked me in I actually get close to the way it felt when I first started pushing around. I remember my first board, my first set of wheels, my Thunder trucks; but then I come down and it rushes away as fast as I can think of it, like a dream. The only way to stay on that wavelength is to keep skating but at forty my body is worn out and my motivation is static, so to supplement all I've been doing lately is trying to write it down and somehow reach that energy through art. Something in me remembers the original urge and the people who motivated me to wanna skate and learn tricks, and then my hair stands on end and I go back in time to when I thought of nothing but that and did nothing but that- it was so fresh. In school I was always antsy to bounce out of class and hop on my board- I couldn't concentrate. Nothing was real except an Ollie, a wallride or a backyard mini ramp or pool.

I destroyed my gear trying all the tricks. My shoes always had duck tape on them or an old, worn out ollie patch; my bearings would always pop and my kingpins would break or my bolts would twist and warp. Skate and Destroy meant my gear, not skate spots. I had to be frugal with my ollies once my socks ripped through and my pinky toe began to bleed. I grew up in *IngleWatts*. Imagine a twelve year-old whiteboy with a freckle-covered face, scraped up knees and a G.I. JOE haircut running wild around the ghetto, and that was me. Our family had just moved to the west side of Inglewood after living by the rugged downtown area since I was a toddler. Our new place was just a mile and a half or so from one of the biggest airports in the entire world: Los Angeles. The city of Angels, which I'm learning means angle, as in arc angle and the actual symmetry required to communicate with Angels.

Over my house was the landing path for LAX and in between jets passing a slipstream zipped through the atmosphere, creating strange sounds like holes ripping through dimensions. Also a loud rumbling that could be mistaken for the end of the world came from planes taking off over the ocean way in the distance. The weird thing is that planes were in the background for so much of my life that the sound actually became a comfort to me.

All around my new neighborhood were skaters. I'd always hear the sound of urethane wheels rolling fast down the sidewalk in front of my house and tried my hardest to see anytime a skater passed. The area was littered with them. Almost everyday the sound of decks crashing on concrete echoed from the school around the corner, taunting me to pick up a skate. A few kids in the area would bring their launch ramps inside and put them up against the handball court to wallride or just fly off them in the open, and on weekends it would turn into a mad session. I'd see skaters on my way to the store, at the pool in the abandoned apartments on La Cienega (where I once saw Ice Cube stopped at the light in a Lexus), or just in the middle of the street doing tricks. I remember always wanting to skate and even had a cheap set up from the swap meet (a ninja board), but I never took it seriously 'til I moved. There weren't any real skaters near my old house, and if anyone did have a board they only rode on their knees or butt with it, or got towed behind a bike. But around my new neighborhood there was a skate culture and dudes that did the *real* shit. When they rolled past my house their wheels would make a loud clack, clack, clack on the sidewalk and I'd watch as they dropped off the curb into the street then ollied up the next. They would inspire kids to skate just by cruising by, and I was on of those kids.

My brothers and sisters (there were seven of us) had their own thing going on so we all did different stuff and never really hung out together as a family. My mom didn't care about what I was doing so I did whatever I wanted. I started skating and following the crowd of skaters in my neighborhood who showed me all the spots, and within a few weeks of moving in it started to take over my life. Soon everything I thought about was in relation to it and slowly the world around me became strictly a place to practice. Driveways were half pipes and the curb cuts off of them were launch ramps. Empty drainage ditches were wonderlands, walls were for riding and red, no parking curbs were for grinding and sliding. My old life was dissolving in front of me. I forgot about everything else. Before skateboarding I was only interested in toys and cartoons, or running around my backyard with motorized squirt guns in a fantasy world. I rode a bike everywhere but had bad luck with it, like flats or a chain that kept breaking 'cuz my bikes were hoopties and always a combination of a lot of bikes, so the parts rarely fit right. Skateboards were less complicated and as it turned out, more addicting. And even though I sucked when I first started skating I somehow knew immediately that I wanted to do it for the rest of my life. It was weird I just connected with it.

It was the perfect outlet for me because my dad was gone, my mom was on welfare and we were broke. Our house was rickety and my brothers and sisters and I grew up wearing shitty clothes and going to church to learn about sin and the return of Jesus. My mom had just relocated us to the more suburban part of Inglewood (if you can imagine one). We moved away from all the crazy bums talking to themselves- the ones I'd cry about to my mom and beg for a dollar from her to give to them.

The irony of moving just as I was entering middle school was that my Jr. high was a quarter block from our old house my entire life, but the year I started going there my mom moves us *two* miles away; it was so far that I ended up going to juvenile hall for being late too much. It was crazy. Lowered Buick Regals cruised up and down the avenues I walked, blaring oldies or the latest rap song, driven by cholos who stuck their shaved heads out the window to see if they scraped on the dips. At the end of the long walk home I'd pass the football field for Inglewood High, Sentinal Field, which was about a half block from my house. All the kids in the neighborhood knew that the local gang held meetings on the bleachers there and they would talk about it as if it was a meeting of super heroes, which was twisted because they were always killing each other.

A few blocks to the west of my house was a huge bridge over the 405 freeway that I always rode my bike across and then another creepy bridge a block south of that for pedestrians only; it was a cage that was at least a hundred feet above the freeway and people only crossed it during the day. The initiation into a crew from the area, The Inglewood Stoners, was to walk across the fenced-over top at night. The bridge was super thin and enclosed with loose fencing that dipped everywhere and was overlooking one of the biggest freeways in the country. With an ocean of red and white lights underneath, being on top almost felt like being in the middle of traffic. One night I crawled halfway across it on a bet thinking I could do it easy and got freaked out and gripped with paralysis by the height. I ended up inching my way backwards and down and then I never went up again- that stuff's not for me.

Just down the street from the bridge near a park is where the Inglewood Stoners hung out. Four of them were brothers (The Mcentees) and the oldest two lived in their mom's garage next door to the local park; so all the other guys came by there too and sometimes they'd all be crowded in the middle of the street drinking beer. A few of them skated and somebody would always be on a board trying tricks. Most of them had long hair and wore ripped up jeans and rocker shirts or denim vests with buttons all over and patches of punk bands sewn onto the back. I skated with the little Mcentee brothers 'cuz we were the same age. We were always getting into trouble somewhere in the neighborhood, or chased when we spied on the older guys having sex with chicks behind the park fence. The Mcentee house was dark and creepy, always crankin' classic rock from a component stereo flanked by two enormous speakers with records strewn everywhere like The Doors, Led Zeppelin and the Rolling Stones and seeds from ganja stuck in every crevice of the house.

I'd see their older brother at the Psycho Bowl up the street, carving the light and he'd always tell me over and over how bad I sucked at skating. I did the tiniest kickturns and probably couldn't stay on my board for more than five seconds. The Inglewood Stoners tagged their crew names in the shallow end down to the last man, but it looked crappy. The Inglewood Skate Rats had way better lettering. They usually tagged IWSR with a roll call underneath it wherever they skated. I'd see it written on walls everywhere I went alongside crude gang tags, etched windows and tags scraped into bus benches.

It was sort of sketchy around my house. I quickly learned to recognize cars that I had to run and hide from, not because I gang banged but because the gangsters didn't care who they harassed or shot at. It helped to know which streets not to go down in bad areas and where the border of Inglewood and Lennox was, as the gangs were at war. Also it helped knowing what candy to bring to the junkies who lived up the block in order to skate an empty pool in their backyard.

I got the shit beat out of me more than once for skating through the wrong area and I constantly found myself jumping fences and ducking through backyards to get out of bad situations. This became so commonplace that I'd never even mention it to my family, and usually after something crazy happened I would walk through the front door like "is there anything for dinner?" But although the neighborhood was unpredictable at times my house was in a safer area than my previous residence downtown, the same way that the Earth is seated in a quiet suburb of the Milky Way. Not too far out though (about five blocks in any direction) it became slightly hostile.

My old residence was in a more dangerous part of Inglewood and I was beginning to get influenced by the neighborhood kids who glorified gangsters; I wanted to wear Khaki pants, slick my hair back (which stubbornly would porcupine) and button my shirt at the top to let the white T show- huero cholo. I remember at lunchtime in the eighth grade watching my friends get jumped into the Jr. version of Inglewood 13, and during their frenzy looking at me to get beat and join the gang. Saying no made me a bitch to them, but somehow, something inside told me to say no even though I secretly wanted to. I could see myself going down the wrong path and becoming too popular with the wrong people. God had different plans for me.

As it turned out most of those guys are now dead or in jail as a direct result of that early initiation. The dude who caused the most trouble on my block, who was the first to be jumped in that day in 8th grade, was hobbling around soon after sporting a full leg cast and bragging about how a rival gang had beat him with an aluminum bat after he threw up his gang's sign. He was barely thirteen. I interpreted this even then as testament to his stupidity and was immediately proud of myself- I could've been dead (and I doubt he's alive).

In my late twenties I learned that time was a physical property that has to be accounted for in scientific experiments. After some digesting of this fact I'd catch myself staring off into the distance at the fuzz in between where I was standing and something far off, knowing I was looking at a slightly different time- the past or the future. The equation of this book requires we go into the past and the math might become distorted, but time travel isn't an exact science.

Today, right now, in my house I'm by myself, it's super lonely and the wind is howling outside causing the waves of foxtails in my backyard to roll and shimmer in the sun. A white sheet over the window is blocking the glare making the whole thing glow like crazy and I'm going over a passage in almost ancient book, The Swindler, from 1554. It says "I think it's a good thing that important events which quite accidentally have never seen the light of day, should be made public and not buried in the grave of oblivion." I feel so close to the author because the hijinx he was involved with as a youngster is the same kind of bullIshit I did when I was a kid; some really cool, some shameful. In a lot of ways his life is like the street skaters that came up in the late 80's, who were mostly all poor (getting into everything). They had to innovate with skateboarding or get sucked into the ghetto- the very real possibility of failure made them work that much harder and the result was a style that was real street life. They saw gangsters and homeless people everywhere they went and skated as fast as they could away from that. It's every skater's story.

The best times I can remember skating were to and from a spot or on the way to the store, or just with no destination in mind; that way it comes down to the terrain and what tricks you can do in the moment, freestyle. This is all I did growing up in Inglewood as a kid with nothing to do but figure out tricks on a plank of wood- like a magician. Throughout my childhood and way into my twenties and thirties I skated with a bunch of different people that motivated and shaped how I progressed. It's bittersweet for me to think about because most of them are missing in action.

One dude I can't get off my mind is a friend I met from upstate New York named Justin. I never realized how much I was into skating until I wrote this. He was a skating legend in the medium-sized town he came from (among other things), and was visiting a friend who had moved all the across the country to Hermosa Beach when we crossed paths. I was 22 and had just dropped out of college. Studies took over my life for a while and it was so intense that I time warped and forgot my skating past during school- but now I was back. After three years of hardly doing it I was making up for lost skate time by practicing all day. Justin thought I was an idiot and had never stopped. He was all about it, with no question in his mind what the optimum position to be held in this world was. Skating was the *only* way for him- I respected that. Everything else in life was just something he did when he wasn't skating. I thought *I* was into it, but here was a fanatic and the more I was around him the more he started to open up about skating, the rules of the game, poetry, chess, everything. The energy of his conversation had me somehow drawn in and the way he talked led you to believe he was older than 21.

He was the kinda guy that saw opportunity in everything that happened to him- on a hot one. He was adjusting well to L.A. but would talk about New York all the time and describe upstate and Long Island incessantly to keep it fresh in his mind. The surfers and longboarders in Hermosa just didn't fit the NYC in his mind and he saw the Strand and all that like it was Disneyland; just a fantasy. I'd listen to him rattle off a few Wu facts like, "There's a place on Long Island called Medina that's supposed to be one of the seven gateways to hell…" In between details his friends would back 'em up, chiming in, "for real kid, you don't want to go there at night." He also quoted Wu-Tang like it was gospel and could attach a profound meaning to all the lyrics, speaking about the members as if they were prophets. When Ghostface's Iron Man was released we all sat around together pondering the lyrics and arguing over the meaning. The guys from New York would catch little nuances that were almost inaudible because the East Coast slang was colloquial and sometimes took a native to understand. I pointed out the innovation in a hip-hop song (Iron Maiden) of a four bar bass that stopped for four bars and began again- everybody thought I was crazy but I was digging it. Mostly we'd talk about skating and he knew underground stories about the pros that I'd never heard. He said that once Tom Penny was at a contest drinking a 40oz on top of a vert ramp and that after he finished it he started doing flip tricks into it from the deck, like nollie backside flip, frontside flip and switch flip, wearing Timberland boots. Only Penny could do something like that.

Justin was just flowing. This excursion to the West Coast was the newest and best chapter in his life. He knew he was in a good spot, saw the skate glitz and smelled how close it was, seeing pros everyday and smoking Kush in beautiful Cali. He had traveled from New York to California years earlier to skate and live in Frisco, but this time he ended up in Hermosa Beach. The way he spoke about staying in SF made me wonder why he came to Hermosa instead. San Francisco is the closest thing city-wise to Long Island, of course with its own flavor. As long as Justin was walking up and down some busy street, he felt at home. Frisco has an unmistakable energy that you start to feel drawing you in like a beacon once you're on the

Golden Gate- you get psyched to skate even if you arrive in the middle of the night. When Tony Bennet sings "I left my heart in San Francisco," he's talking about something magnetic everyone experiences after visiting SF. Nothing comes close to Frisco. It's physics, and you can't do shit about that.

Hermosa could pass for a movie-set version of SF. Pier Avenue back in the day was like a miniature Haight Street with so many hippie kids everywhere barefoot and all the people stoned. Someone who had never seen it before could easily get hooked on it, especially back then- way before it was bourgeoee. He made it sound like he had no choice but to leave New York, like he was running from drug dealers or the mob or he was hiding from the police. He wasn't going back there and if anything he would migrate to Frisco. On a bus from N.Y. making his way to L.A., he read a book on chess strategy and whipped our asses every day playing and could apply the same strategy to s.k.a.t.e.

He could skate better drunk than sober and once showed up to Hermosa Pier with his girl and beat everyone there, one after the other, making fun of us the whole time. Starting with tre-flip, nollie backside flip, something in the middle of that and a switch hardflip. I could smell his breath five feet away. He was invincible in Sal Barbier 23s (a classic Etnies shoe), doing every trick and making his exit by 360 flipping the four-stair next to the ledge- along with a backside and frontside flip- and laughing as he picked up his board and walked off holding his chick's hand. He might've even called us losers as he melted into the crowd. We all wanted another chance at a game to win but he wasn't gonna let that happen.

His stories from New York were so smooth you could tell they had been told dozens of times like rehearsed monologues. They were experiences that pulled you away like you lassoed a comet, involving running from drug dealers he owed money to; owning a skate shop (and selling weed out of it); living by himself on Long Island at an early age; getting flowed by Lance Mountain (Firm owner); showing up pros at demos in his hometown, and the list went on. He was way ahead of his time when he met Lance. They were skating a famous tiled bank in upstate and Justin was doing nollie big spin heels and other tricks that caught his attention. His friends said to me, staring straight into my eyes, "he did it all kid". Running from drug dealers wasn't a main concern of his (although he owed a guy for a few pounds of weed) because his dad was a DEA agent. He went out of his way to make sure everybody knew it; this gave him an elevated view of the law because he realized it was just who you knew that determined whether the law applied. This gave him more confidence than most 21 year olds.

He didn't care about shit- he just wanted to skate and smoke ze chronic. Nobody in the South Bay was that dedicated to skating except the local pros, so he kind of shook everyone up- even them. He worked during the day and filmed at night or on his days off, getting sick clips like long fakie 5-0s to shuv at the baggage claim (L.A.X.), long lines at the beach, tricks at Beryl. He was coming up everywhere.

Any time he talked about skating his friends were always backing up what he was saying by their confident nodding. Mostly his stories would start with: "Who remembers when…" And then he went on from there about some antics back home or something about a pro's career, hardly letting anyone else talk. The East Coast was blowing up and he had a lot to say about it. Three of his buddies tagged along from New York, showing up after he got situated, one by one. They all stayed in the same apartment and seemed close like they'd known each other their whole life, but when it got real it was definitely every man for himself. Brian was the most loyal and his closest friend- like a puppy dog. Out of all of them he was my favorite; there was just something so human about him. He told everybody everything and never held back- the dude was super likeable, always ready to film and down for any skater. He had lived with Justin ever since they moved out of their houses in New York. The friendship they all had was cool because nobody expected anything from anyone else except to corroborate a story they might be telling or listen to the description of a trick. It was refreshing. Mostly Justin would be talking, and as he would tell a story about skating or whatever his buddies would just chime in details.

All of them had Wu-Tang on the brain; the subject would be either Wu-Tang or skating. And clothes. When they weren't skating they wanted to wear Timberland boots (if possible) and break up sticky ass weed to roll into blunts. These luxuries were all inconsistent but we dreamed of a day when we had an endless sack. They had heavy East Coast accents and everything they said ended in *yo* or *kid*. You could tell them anything. Nothing was crazy or embarrassing, and without hesitation they would express what was on their mind. That was new to me. Once near the bars in Hermosa I was running my fingers along on a window like a miniature skater as we walked and Brian said, "every skater does that." I wasn't even aware I was ollieing from window to window and smiled looking at him while I front crook'd the next frame. Once in college my girlfriend caught me doing that to her tits using them as banks. We were laying down and she looked at me and said "you skating on my boobs."

We'd walk and skate all over the place, and when it started getting late we'd search for weed. Forgetting where we were going from talking so much. Justin would tell stories he'd heard about his favorite skaters like Jeremy Wray or Sean Mullendore (who's abilities were other worldly in his eyes). He'd name amazing tricks they'd done or magazine photos of them, squinting his eyes and shaking his head no like, 'what were they thinking when they did that trick.' Then he'd close his lips and very slowly say pfffffffffewww. He'd name East Coast spots like Palowski Park and constantly ask me if I'd heard of it. When I said no he'd sound so surprised and say 'I can't believe you've never heard of Palowski.' Koston and Guy's parts in *Mouse* were as mind blowing as the riddle of the Sphinx and the constellations to them. It was like they were mythical figures born out of some volcano and given super powers. I understood their zeal because I felt exactly the same way- there was nothing like it.

This included Daewon. Once at Torrance High, Justin and his buddy Kyle watched as Dae filmed a switch nose grind to fakie flip out across an entire ledge, hitting it dead on. While he was in between tries they leaned over and murmured the trick to each other like a couple of pro golf announcers commenting on a near perfect stroke. Justin could go on forever about videos like *Mouse* and knew all about the *Eastern Exposure* series. He'd especially get goin' when the blunt was being rolled and passed. His friends would bring up something that happened in New York or a legendary skate vid as the opening act for a story Justin would take control of like a young Henry Miller, correcting details they mishandled and telling his version- the best one. An epiphany would turn into a completely developed idea that he would dispose of at random. He would talk like he was in a trance, and what was presently going on around us didn't even register; he'd look right through people walking by like they were ghosts.

Anybody that did anything too much he would label *the master* of doing that, and when I would crooked grind everything in a session he'd say "Gayton's the crooked grind *master*". Belittling his good friends was no problem. It came natural to him. Because hardly anything excited him, everyone busted up when he laughed and when he did, his voice erupted like it was pent up for months, waiting to explode.

One day I brought them all to Beryl Street banks in Redondo. They skated the steep side to see how hard the tricks were that Daewon had done on it, and they hit it a few times almost not trying so that the difficulty of the pro's tricks became even more legendary. Justin asked after a few times rolling up the bank: "How the fuck did they skate this shit?" He completely got into it and looked so confused when he hit the bank, with a look on his face like 'what were these mad geniuses thinking.' They were obviously mad men. I was so psyched to hear such hype talk about skating that I just stood back and absorbed the vibe because it backed up the feelings I already had for it. The conversation turned to Henry Sanchez as they stood staring at the steep part shaking their head in amazement, periodically saying in an East Coast accent "soooo sick." You can tell they had a deep respect for skateboarding and didn't for a second question it's future as being anything but the next sport to enter the world stage. Justin was their nominee for pro status and the conversation inevitably turned to what trick he could do at Beryl. Anytime he mentioned to his buddies the trick he was thinking of, anywhere we were they would say "that'd be so sick kid," while he stared at the spot in deep contemplation, nodding slowly. They all had complete faith in him.

When he wasn't around his friends would tell stories about him. They'd talk in a super serious tone that exalted his exploits and added to his legend and start like they were narrating a movie. They'd first look around as if a crime was being committed, then start in on an epic. Sometimes after hearing these tales I would say "is that story for real?" Or "is Justin that good of a skater?" They'd roll their eyes and invariably respond, "no doubt." Then they would get a serious look on their face and say something about his skating to back it up that usually started with "once back in New York…" Their energy contributed to his skills. They almost lifted him up in the air the way they kissed his ass.

One rainy night when we were trying to find some place to skate, we saw Rodney Mullen at the L.A.X. baggage claim. Justin was skating with him for a while and started up a conversation about hardflips. Rodney was doing huge switch hardflips and began explaining the movement to Justin while his friends watched. Within two or three tries he landed it. Brian's eyes lit up and quickly reduced the attempts to first try saying "oh my god, that kid's a natural." After that they talked about seeing Rodney forever. And I guess that's pretty sick- I would too if I was them. He just popped into the Matrix. These guys travelled to California to see the pros and here was the top of the top. They all tripped out at the rumors of Marcus Mcbride switch backside tailsliding one of the benches inside the baggage claim days later (I think it was an ad) saying, "that spot's blowing up!" For them skating was the main course, nothing else piqued their interest. It was the first time I ever heard skateboarding being talked about in such a way. I needed to hear it too because their enthusiasm focused and motivated me. After a few years in college I woke up like 'what was I thinking' and felt like I'd missed out on an amazing era in just three years. That's why I was later motivated by Rodney when I started filming him; age didn't mean shit to the guy and it still doesn't.

Skating was so different back then. You had to live it in the late nineties to understand how inspired it was- writing about it only brings it back for a second (Epicly Later'd gets a lot closer than this could). In a way it's like the hippie's in San Francisco during the 60's. Almost every video had heart and the pros were taking skating in an unknown direction that we all uncritically followed as gospel. Justin was part of it, bringing the East

Coast to Cali. He was a character. I saw how he worked the world; hearing him tell his stories helped me see the value of my own experiences. He personified the saying 'in the land of the blind the one-eyed man is king'. The dude always kept slightly ahead of his crew at all times- enough to keep them in awe and following him.

Hermosa Beach is where we mostly hung out. We always stayed out around the strand so late that the streetlights began to look like constellations making the ocean spray glow as we skated. Usually we played a game of skate for hours 'til none of us could skate. It got late fast as we lost track of time and talked our asses off until the bars were out and the streets were empty, about hip hop, skating or some scary place in New York. I paid more attention to skate related stuff than anything taught to me in college.

The last time I saw Justin was when I dropped him off in front of a hotel in SF with his exotic chicki, Jessica, who migrated from New York to be with him. She had him under some kind of hypnotic trance and with a kind of wicked smile she would make requests, almost driving him crazy with her demands. Skating definitely took a back seat when she came through. I wanted to bring them there because for a while I'd been meaning to visit and skate SF. It's all I've ever heard about from any serious skater. Plus, I knew Justin and I could film some cool shit there or skate some sick spots- whatever. I just wanted to see it. They were ditching out on rent at an apartment close to the beach that we all used to hang out at drinking, smoking and acting a fool. Sometimes there'd be ten or so of us packed in there. As the headlining act at night Justin and Jessica would disappear into their bedroom about 2 a.m. when nobody was paying attention. Then we'd hear them through the wall mumbling things to each other, moaning in unison then back to the mumbling. We would all sit uncomfortably trying to change the subject, which was no use as anything we tried to put our mind to was upstaged by their moaning. They had used the place up and rent was way past overdue when Justin made the decision to leave.

One day he asked me to meet him around back of the place where he could load his suitcases into my car and not be seen by the landlady. I pulled into the parking garage and began looking around for him when he stealthily appeared from behind a few cars, suitcase in hand. We loaded the car up and after Jessica jumped in we started out to SF, which was going to be a one-way trip for them, as they had no friends left in Hermosa or any other options except to ask for their parents to wire them more money. I couldn't see Justin getting a job in Frisco (although he had one in Hermosa before Jessica arrived) because he had to keep tabs on his girl. Their relationship made them both unable to see clearly, and it turned into an obsession- especially with all the dudes after her in Hermosa. At this point they were just looking for resources to sustain their addiction for each other and at the moment I was a resource.

We started out on our trip at 8 p.m. and after a few hours made it through the grapevine and across the cow country leading to SF where the gnarly stench of manure was almost unbearable. It was especially pronounced because Jessica wouldn't shut up about it. She was not only irritated by the smell but kept asking me over and over why I couldn't fix a rattling my car was making.

Eventually she went to sleep and the rattling began to sound heavenly in contrast to her complaining. Justin and I kept smoking joints all the way up and both of us took turns at the wheel during the long stretch of the 5. Just before I left my house that day to pick up Justin I stopped by a friends who had just thrown out a huge pot plant, harvested early because he was sketching out about the landlord. It was good luck that I came by 'cuz he had just trashed the thing. He told me that he might have left some buds on it, so I dug it out of his dumpster in the alley and was able to peel a half-ounce off. It was immature but still far enough along to work well and ended up being a grip, lasting us almost the whole trip. It helped on the long, boring drive while we listened to the same mix tape over and over 'til we just turned it off.

Once we started across the Golden Gate Justin spotted the place where Kalis had a photo ollieing over a rail with the ocean in the background (that I didn't see 'til it was reprinted years later). He got inspired and began to talk about the times he lived in SF and also the famous spots and skaters. After crossing the bridge, we stopped at Embarcadero and in the early morning hours with hardly any light he and I ran around the place to relive all the most amazing tricks done there. He knew everything Carrol and Lavar did as well obscure pros and tricks- he was a fanatic. The security box was still standing in the middle of the place but the popularity of the spot had long fizzled out and nobody skated it anymore. Justin's enthusiasm about the stories made them seem like the most important events in history- and the pros and ams that lived it will tell you it *was*.

We drove through the wharf into the Tenderloin and the whole scene made me think of Del and Hieroglyphics, then through the red light district where we got lost 'til the sun came up. Later in the day when we were almost dizzy from driving he pointed out the double-sided curbs where most of Danny Sargant's part from the New Deal video (Useless Wooden Toys) was filmed; he knew obscure stuff. The skate life was second nature to him.

We ate at a breakfast place just next to Fort Miley that overlooked the ocean way down below. We drank a bunch of coffee to wake up and when I excused myself to use the bathroom Justin blurted out, "Someone's gotta take a shit". After breakfast we walked down to see the ocean from a lookout point near the entrance of the nature reserve. It was April and the wind was making the dark blue water choppy; the spray from the crashing waves was misting us from down below. Somewhere out there I was sure were Great Whites patrolling; there were dozens of surfers out on the water that morning that knew this and didn't give a fuck. A friend told me that surfers out here were sometimes scared shitless by kelp that was forced under by the waves then thrust to the surface by the giant air bulbs that suspended them, causing a violent burst that the surfer would momentarily think was a shark.

After that we visited and skated Fort Miley where Justin talked about all the tricks done on the bank to rail and over the pyramid. He was like an encyclopedia of skating. The air was crisp and smelled like the pine trees surrounding the skate spot, which sits high above the nature reserve. The proximity from the city cut out the noise pollution and the lack of sound interference was deafening. I was juiced on the trip but seemed to be injecting all the enthusiasm as Justin and Jessica were preoccupied, which you could hardly blame them for. They had to figure out how they were going to survive in SF and tried to hide it by molesting each other and making out all over the place, maintaining a cool confidence the whole time. Jessica constantly called Justin over to talk alone and get reassurance. While he was comforting her I skated the banks, which were steep and hard to get used to. The pyramid in the middle jerked me hard when I hit it and any trick done on it immediately increased tenfold in value.

   Later in the day we visited the Deluxe shop. Justin saw James Kelch outside as we pulled up (he could spot random people out of nowhere and knew where everything in SF was). We went in and looked around for a while at all the new Spitfire and Real designs. I bought a Spitfire shirt and a set of 50mm wheels while Justin was kissing Jessica and molesting her as he whispered things in her ear, which she replied to playfully, "noooooo". I watched him dominate her and deep inside it activated my ego that later is what led me to do this with girls I was dating.

The trip was completely impromptu with no plan whatsoever- or not one I was in on- we were just lurking around. After leaving the shop we drove around some more and got out to skate a few times kind of lost and confused about what to do. I went off skating on my own and found a bunch of black marble blocks and saw a few skaters, but we were far from Pier 7. It was only my second time in SF and I didn't know anyone. It's the ideal skate/art city. Everyone loves the vibe. Weed is cheap there and the kindest in the world is easily procured, it's the original couchlock. The hippies never left and you could get the best shrooms as well and easily find a peaceful forest setting within city limits to trip out in.

After some long disappearances by Justin and Jessica- where they left me waiting in the car perplexed and irritated by their shadiness- they returned and said they needed to get their bags. Justin took me aside and explained to me that he and Jessica got a hotel room and that, basically, she didn't want me around. He tried to say sorry but I told him not to, because inside I was secretly relieved as the whole situation was getting old and as usual, skating took a back seat. I knew it was a bad situation and our trip was starting to suck. At the time I was only concerned about skate progression and couldn't understand or get into the mind of anyone that wasn't thinking the same way.

Justin had, momentarily at least, given up skating to focus on Jessica. I had long sensed some sort of addiction between the two that prevented any genuine living, only a fevered obsession with each other. He felt bad for leaving and gave me some gas money, and after grabbing all their stuff we said goodbye. I haven't seen him since. I never really heard the exact details about what happened to them except they broke up and both had to move back to New York. They got back together a few times 'til they both fucked up so much that their relationship couldn't recover.

Justin was the first real skateboarding fanatic I'd ever met. He understood that the utility of the board merged with the art and simply cruising down the street made you a better skater. Just after he got me to put skateboarding first, the feeling started to go away in him (like an energy looking for a new host) and his relationship with Jessica became all consuming. From the few stories I did hear their love degraded into insanity and became a mostly drunken mania of fights and breakups- her sleeping with his best friends and all sorts of shit.

Years past and I kept skating, eventually moving to Long Beach. My skating gained different dimensions because of the move and I needed the change- all the new obstacles made me think of different tricks. It's like I had new room to stretch my legs. It took months to explore just a small part of the city. The downtown area around the LB Library (a place we called Bum Park) and near the fountain off of Pine is by itself a mission to explore. I got that same, 'brand new' feeling years later after coming off of skateboard tours- like my whole life had been refreshed. For weeks after tour I would just be jazzed and felt like everything in life was new- I guess the feeling of traveling was too good (and it's still with me, fresh like yesterday). There were some tours that were especially memorable and I remember trying to emulate that feeling the pros seemed to have being psyched with their position and status (doing demos and getting all the attention and photos in the mags), and just buzzed overall from the excitement of filming, skating and getting paid. Having caught the skate bug again years after I went away from it, I wondered why I had stopped to begin with. I actually regretted it big time. My crazy home life growing up has a lot to do with it. Now that I was back at it I tried to forget going to college because I wanted to go back in time and drop out to only skate. Those long afternoons in lecture halls and endless nights doing countless math problems that I can't remember for shit seemed worthless like a robbery of my youth. But who knows where I would've been mentally if I didn't go to school (it's weird). Later I read a quote from a famous historian saying that people aren't ready for college 'til thirty, and I totally agree. The words "rejoice in thy youth o young man," aren't instructing you to spend your early twenties paying massive amounts of money to learn revisionist history and Chinese math (although I loved geometry). The worst part about college is the stress everyone feels to achieve faster and get a degree quicker. Most talk on college campuses is actually about transferable credits and GPAs instead of intellectual stuff.

It took me years to get out of that mindset of regret and be thankful for college and that I had a good mind that could see. As I get older I understand more and more that this was the analytical upgrade that helped me appreciate skateboarding; so much so that I ditched college to skate, which was the only decision to make in hindsight. Once I started to analyze skating I never stopped. I was accused of being a slacker (one of my favorite films) but leaving school eventually helped me travel a grip, filming some of the best pros in the world and getting paid. And all of this I owe to the Inglewood Skate Rats.

2

Yesterday I walked out of my house and up the slope of my front yard to the street about to hop on my skateboard heading toward the intersection. Just then, and I mean no sooner than the street came into view, a skater dipping into the crosswalk flew off his board and landed upside down right in front of my eyes. He hit a curb cut wrong on a downhill riding a ridiculously small 70s board, and it chucked him causing this hippy looking dude to arc weirdly from about four feet up straight onto his neck immediately going unconscious. It was fucking surreal! He instantly started convulsing and helplessly jerking on the hot asphalt with the sun blaring on him. Watching from across the street I was stunned and frozen like almost everybody seeing it. All the cars just stopped and a bunch of them pulled over to help, blocking the crosswalk all around him to prevent eager drivers from squeezing past. They were all on their cell phones calling 911 when he woke up and screamed, "HELP ME!!" a few times in a desperate, angry, panicked state of complete shock. An older man told him to stay down multiple times as he was trying to get up over and over, only able to lift his head a few inches while making a terrible wailing noise with constrained airways that sounded like someone expressing the worst pain possibly imaginable to a human being! He was straight up screaming. The ambulance was taking a while and everybody was anticipating the sirens. I didn't want to see anything else and it started to feel gnarly watching so when they did come I bailed. The paramedics passed me on my way down the hill and made a right on PCH toward Kaiser hospital.

I always wondered what happened to the dude and told the story to almost everyone I came into contact with for the next few days trying to figure out the meaning of what I'd seen, if there was any. I wished him the best then hopped on the bus after carefully skating to the stop so I could get to the skatepark.

While I was cruising down PCH the bus ride brought back memories of treks I'd take from Inglewood to any number of skate spots, sometimes with George or Shorty (my Skate Rat friends), other times just by myself. When I did go with those guys it was a skate lesson. George lived closest to me growing up and was the most gifted of the Inglewood Skate Rats. His body was built strictly for skating, which he almost took for granted he had so much natural ability. Little Horhito was the phenomenon in IWSR, as he was their prodigy who far surpassed any expectations. He put in mega work but the practice was just natural progression with almost no attempts and only lands. Every trick he did was done the right way, effortlessly, and served as instruction for how it should look, nailing it over and over to keep it.

He was always pushing the envelope and seemed to be tapped into the skateboarding zeitgeist. The first time I met him he was boardsliding a double-sided curb and rock and rolling off, (as it had no end) behind the Hostess thrift store on Manchester. He was wearing ET surf sweats and laughing as he slid it every time, angling the board slightly further back to give it style. The curb was slick as hell and when I boardslid it I flew back onto my hand and was impaled by a dried plant stem sticking out of the dirt. The cut was so deep it looked like it had green stuff coming out of it along with white chunks of flesh; I was scared to do boardslides for a while after that. George always laughed about that.

Watching George skate so effortlessly made you wonder whether he ever injured himself at all because I never saw him fall, really, just bail tricks. He must've been born in a perfect celestial alignment, whereas I felt like I was born just behind the correct one, stuck in a swirling soup of unstable elements.

All these memories make a smile appear on my face that must've made me look crazy to the other passengers. The bus driver is hauling ass and we keep jerking and swaying as he makes the stops. We all wobble a bit and the people standing hold on to the railings extra tight so they don't fly forward or end up in someone's lap. I gave my seat up near the front for an older lady just getting on and stood with everyone else. The bus I was on cruised down through Redondo Beach passing Aviation blvd. where ET Surf is. When I was just a little grom I'd travel there to buy clothes or boards after I made money at the aquarium. On their wooden counter were pictures of the Inglewood Skate Rats in plastic frames. I'd see photos of

Mikey and Chris Elder who were the older members, and maybe George as well. Shorty was absent from the frames because he rode for Santa Monica Airlines and Rip City Skates was his home shop. It was way out in Santa Monica where George and I went with him a bunch of times to get boards and stuff from Skip Englomb. George got World Industries boards from Jesse Martinez and always wore E.T. Surf sweatpants or shorts. He rode Jesse's mini-model, as he was so young and compact, and had *Skinny Little Whiteboy* neon colored rails like two parenthesis on the bottom. Making his board look sick were Gizmo wheels where Shorty had OJs or Bullets- because SMA was part of Santa Cruz and his packages said NHS (little details only a skate nerd would know)- which made his board look like a stomper truck as they were thin and tall.

If we were lucky we got a ride to skate spots from a few older dudes that had cars, otherwise we took the bus like it was no big thing. Most car rides I remember involving skating were trips to abandon pools that the older guys were super into. A few times Chris brought music and we blasted Ice Cube's *Amerika's Most Wanted* out of the cassette deck on the way. Mostly a guy named Big Al drove us around (a school teacher that was an o.g. member). The Skate Rats also had a member that was a mailman, and on his routes he'd scope abandoned or recently vacated houses and apartments for empty pools and let the other dudes know where they were. If it was legit and skateable they'd show up with their fat Aggressor knee pads and session it secretly. I remember so many times when I was a kid peeking into backyards looking for the dry oasis of an empty pool and the excitement I felt seeing one, especially if it had perfect transitions and was shaped decently. Showing up to a secret pool and hearing the riding from behind the walls on the way in before seeing anything always got my heart pumping.

In my neighborhood there was the Kidney Pool and the Psycho Bowl. The very first time I encountered the Skate Rats they were shredding the Psycho bowl (which was actually a square pool with tranny'd out corners). They were on it that day, killin' it, hitting tile, grinding the hip, carving the shallow end and feeding off each-others energy tag-team style. There was huge crowd that day. A skater never forgets the first time they witness real shredding. I specifically remember Shorty that day wearing Chuck Taylors with the high top section folded down and black socks with black laces. He always wore a chain and hat, and looked way odd hatless at school. Later when I got to know him I realized how much of a character he was and also that he was a snake on the ramp. On the local minis we skated he would, over and over, do frontside airs then grab his nose and land to tail while everyone waited on the deck for their run. Again and again after an axle stall he'd do the trick (and stall forever) like none of them were satisfying enough, until eventually even he grew tired of it and would mercifully let someone else skate. Shorty was the kinda guy who'd play the same song over and over 'til you hated him: "My name is D-NICE… taking out you suckas and you don't know how I did it" over and over again, playing the extended single cassette version. I couldn't understand why he'd play the song out like that, until I progressed into my own style later in life. Now when I get into a song I play it 'til I can't hear it again just thinking about my skating, like Maurice Payne (a.k.a. Shorty).

We both went to Inglewood High in ninth grade and I'd always see him between classes or at lunch. He led a double life in between skating and I don't know what he did, but if I called his name at school when he was hanging out with friends, one of his buddies would correct me saying, "no no, this ain't Shorty, this Dre-bop." In Jr. high he would confiscate my board when I'd see him at lunch and start skating in between the basketball and handball players. Once he hopped on my board and did a kickflip then hit a crail snatcher on the gym wall like it was nothing, wearing new *Levis* and a button up *Gucci* shirt. He had steeze. The Skate Rats were a rare group. The skills they had led you to believe in the *natural* rather than understanding the actual work that they put in way before I started skating. As an example I'd see Mikey at Payne Elementary practicing by himself all the time when I was a kid, doing all the new shuv-its and ollieing big shit. He would just progress on his own, regardless of anyone else. Like the time I saw Guy Mariano at World Park, about '92 before he had his growth spurt, practicing half cab heel flips to fakie on a quarter pipe until he did two huge ones in a row, with only one other person around.

Mikey lived near Payne and would be happy to see other skaters session the school ('cuz we were rare in the late 80's and back then all skaters were bros). Not trying to impress anyone but the universe, he was just skating and wasn't expecting anyone to show up. He always wore shorts and his shins were fucked; there wasn't an inch of them that didn't have a scar. The dude was a giant and he always had a smile on his face like he was masking something deeper and afraid to be depressed; like he had a few experiences in the ghetto that were terrible and never wanted to see the dark side again, so he only thought about positive stuff to fight off the bad energy, skating as fast as he could to escape any reminder of it. Or maybe he just knew how good he was at skating and this was a sign of his satisfaction.

I remember once he was doing shuv-it pivot reverts on flat- the board just rotating smoothly every direction on the ground like a helicopter blade- and something sick on the small hips that were a foundation for a trailer. He skated like he expected the board to be there and never thought of not landing on it- his body was just leaning in a forward direction as he attacked the spot. Mikey was definitely a factor in L.A.'s skate progression because skaters multiplied exponentially thereafter and here was the square root. One day at Payne his friend brought along a Polaroid and I got a flick of a melon grab over the hip because the guy snapping flicks was cool enough to show a little love. That was about the only documentation we got back then- all skating was live, the real state of the art was only seen by a few people. I still have an old Polaroid of me doing a chink-chink on a parking block we set on top of a mini ramp. The photo came out dark because it was inside an abandoned warehouse in Ladera Heights. We constructed it using stolen plywood and skated the thing everyday 'til the cops ripped it up. In the photo my friend Gary is standing on the deck holding his Natas board in the background, protecting his shins with it like a shield.

Mikey was always in the car scrunched together with all of us sweaty, stinking skaters on the way to some spot. He seemed upbeat and involved and always led the discussion when the older dudes were talking, so it was a shock to me when I saw him enraged in meltdown mode. One day he came out of his house on fire, fighting with his mom as we all waited, packed in a car in the summer heat to take off to some spot. She wouldn't let him go skate and we could hear her throwing a conniption fit inside! It was strange to see such a giant (Mikey was hella tall) get punked by his mom, but she was threatening to kick him out and put all of his shit on the curb if he left with us. We kept urging him to just go anyways. We told him she wouldn't do it and getting courage from us he psyched himself up to confront his mom and returned inside, which was a disaster. This time the yelling got worse and we heard more objects fly and stuff break inside until his board came flying over the gate, so that all we saw from the car was a board flying out of nowhere and crashing on the cement just in front of us. Then he appeared with a psychotic look on his face, pacing back and forth and raging to himself about what *'bullshit'* it was. George and I were so insensitive we laughed. Mikey gave us the craziest look and for a second I was scared he'd drag us out of the car and beat the shit out of us!

We ended up having to leave without him. I kept a smile on my face as we drove away because I was ashamed to be such an asshole in such a sensitive situation. By laughing we were expressing that undisciplined side of skating that lacked respect for anything and cancelled all loyalties the instant there was an opportunity for a joke or a chance to take out a hidden, unwanted feeling on someone else. Most skaters I knew were rotten and the only reason we were able to skate anywhere in the city, at any time with whoever, was because our parents didn't care where we were. With no supervision anything goes so that wild, obnoxious side develops, unchecked. It insured that we didn't fit in anywhere. Any opportunity to adapt to mainstream life was quickly soiled by this animal side. Later in life *I* would even be annoyed by these loud packs of crazy kids that I failed to recognize as me years ago. It's just a way of masking being unwanted- a paradox. It's the terrible urge to laugh at a friend when he needs you most like we did to Mikey.

Despite all of our shortcomings we still came together to live the skate life. We first watched Ray Barbee kickflip pivot a bank to bench in *Public Domain* at Mikey's house, (one of the vids that changed my life). It was one night after skating and we sat in his living room with our hats sticking to our foreheads and salt in the eyes. I remember being so psyched on the trick like I had just discovered an alien race, and what I thought was possible had just flown out the window. For the next hour I became completely unaware of my existence, like an out of body experience. Something inexplicable came over all of us as our jaws dropped, tapping parts of the mind left dormant for just such information; not one of us said a word to each other throughout the entire video, just a lot of 'damns'. I was too young at the time to analyze skating; I was just super into it.

Nobody there was thinking about the future as we watched the video, we were just lost in the skateboarding dream. What really sucked was that hardly any of us had the stability and security at home to support the skate life that resulted in a Ray Barbee (I don't even know how he did it). The reasons and signs were there; in the ghetto almost every residence and family is transient, just like mine, and bound to move around from city to city. Sometimes without your group of friends for encouragement to skate, moving means quitting. Especially if there weren't supportive parents involved or places to skate and progress; and the only skateparks in existence back then were Carlsbad and Tijuana. Most of us had to get a job as soon as we turned 16.

Shorty already had a job. He was always busy cleaning buildings at night with his 'boss' or chasing some girl during the day. He had preternatural confidence and would look at you crazy if you told him he should be skating, not working. He felt like he always needed money. A few times at school I saw him in the principles office for fighting, or I ran into him on the streets near campus hanging out with entire squads of black dudes that would talk shit to me until Shorty told them to chill. Despite his inner-drive and talent, the ghetto just absorbed him eventually. He was an adult way before he was a kid.

Once when I visited his house to go skate he answered the door with his finger pointing up over his lips shoooshing me as his father was asleep on the floor. He nudged his dad asking him to borrow the car. His Dad then handed the keys to Shorty like 'don't bother me' and rolled over back to sleep. So Shorty drove us to the store in a Cadillac- we were only fifteen, but he looked a little older 'cuz he had a peach fuzz mustache. We came back and he cooked steak before we skated while his pop was still asleep shirtless on the floor. He kept shooshing me to insure his pop would stay asleep. The dude was was always shooshing me, that was his thing. If anyone said something stupid he would just stop them by putting his finger over his mouth and saying 'sssshhhh', and when they kept trying to interject he would just keep shaking his head shooshing. This made everyone mad 'cuz they didn't know what he was doing; but he didn't give a fuck. Dre-Bop would talk shit to anyone.

He eventually quit skating like all of the Skate Rats did. It sucks when that happens but, except for very few, stopping is inevitable. Almost fifteen years later a friend of mine, SAD, said that Shorty had somehow resurfaced asking his former sponsor, Skip Englomb, if he could move in with a girl he got pregnant. A few too many of his plans had unraveled, I'm guessing, which was easy 'round here. The pressure to succeed in Los Angeles is so great that one wrong move could break you.

Shorty would always be at the bank to chain behind Savon Drugs not too far from his house. It was one of the only good spots around so that was where I'd go after school hoping to meet up with him (but a lot of pros knew about it too). Out of nowhere one day after I had just got there, Scott Oster came through right when I thought I was gonna skate by myself the whole time. He showed up with his buddy in a red Nissan *Sentra*. They popped the trunk and said 'what's up' and almost right away I recognized Scott from seeing him in the magazines. He started carving up the bank using the parking block like a lip, hitting it surfer style with his ponytail whipping around, looking back slightly. There was a bandana tied around his head like a kamakazi pilot and he wore shades to protect his eyes that seemed to be allergic to the sun. Immediately I started talking to him and asking questions. He saw the shuv-its and no-complys I was doing (from watching *Shackle Me Not*) and seemed interested, asking me what they were and trying to do them, so I tried extra hard to bust them all out. His set up was shiny and there were Dogtown stickers covering the graphic next to silver Independent stickers overlapping each other and even sticking over the base plate of his trucks. I told him about a local mini ramp I knew about and before he left we made plans to skate it.

I got his number and would call him every time I was headed to the bank to chain hoping he'd show up. It was sort of unbelievable for a kid from the ghetto to be hanging out with a pro like that and seeing everything close up, but that's how the pros were back then, really supportive. It'd always be after school when I'd hit 'em up to see if he was skating and I'd push super far through sketchy neighborhoods to meet up with him. Once I showed up with a bloody face after just being jumped *bad* for skating down the wrong street. There was a short cut to Ladera Heights up a few hills that were in unknown territory and I was caught off guard by Piru Bloods who came out of nowhere, asking me why I had a red shirt on and what school I went to. Before I could even think, they just started beating the shit out of me, busting my eyebrow open and ringing my head, causing me to see double for a second! I backed up as fast as I could, jumped on my board and used the hill to escape, hoping I wouldn't get the wobbles. Just before I ran away one of them started grabbing at the back of his waist like he had a gun and I knew it was time to book it, so with tears running down my face I used all the energy I had to bomb the hill ducking a little in case he did have a gun. It sucked. From then on I went way around to avoid that area. When I met up with Scott he seemed super bummed that my face was so messed up and the session was kind of quiet. Coming from Westchester and always driving it probably seemed foreign to him, but it was something I dealt with everyday.

We skated a lot after that and soon I bugged him for a board. He said he had a bunch a gear for sale and told me if I brought some friends to his house to buy some skate stuff, he'd give me a deck. A few days later I showed up by myself and told him my friends weren't around. The truth is that I didn't ask anybody and just wanted a board. He let me in his house and brought me to a room that was filled wall to wall with skate gear, like it was gonna flood into the living room if the door stayed open too long. Scott just looked at me and asked me what board I wanted. The room smelled like new product and looked like an ancient king's treasure room to me, glowing with boards bursting out of the treasure chests and stickers water falling in front; wheels everywhere, shirts, trucks, rails, hardware- thrown anywhere they fit, and on top of that. In his backyard he had a collection of every board he ever rode- a lot of them cracked in half. The layout of the house and all the space he had made it a perfect skate headquarters. He gave me so many stickers that I covered the whole board and even put them in between the grip tape on the front. I felt sponsored and Scott told me he was gonna talk to the Dogtown TM to put me on as am, but already his relations with them were starting to sour. I could tell he wanted to adjust to the new style and I acted as a sort of muse with the tricks I was doing. He was already on track but the drastic changes taking place in skating happened almost overnight and caught everyone off guard. We skated a lot after that and I got some exposure to some big name pros at an early age, like Christian Hosoi, Pat Ngoho and Eric Dressen, but after he left Dogtown I hardly saw him or heard from him.

Recently in an anthropology book I read that 'great Soviet minds of the cold war era turned to chess instead of signing up to engineer weapons for the military'. I feel the same about skaters, like they were the thwarted rocket scientists that, given the choice between flying to the moon or flying off a launch ramp they chose skating and saw it as the only pursuit worth their time (because it's right in front of you). Rodney Mullen has a degree in physics and can't stop skating, like the physics knowledge only added more clarity to the skating. He's a skater that applies science to the building of new skate products. I remember he talked on and on about P.J. Ladd's skate part in *Wonderful*

Horrible Life as if it was a cutting edge scientific discovery. For a while everybody we ran into at the office or at a spot would hear about P.J.'s part from Rodney. A real fan of the sport that also enjoyed having his mind blown by other skaters- that's what keeps him loyal to the sport. The way he described skating to me when I filmed him was precise and technical and altogether could have easily constituted a Euclid textbook of skateboarding. He'd turn an empty parking lot into a living movie of skateboarding's history and with subtle movements of his hands he'd paint images in the air that I swear were visible and clear. We'd lose a lot of daylight that way.

My reminiscing ended when the bus reached my stop so I got off and headed up the street to the Wilmington skatepark. There's four blocks to skate to get there through a sketchy area. About a block away from the skatepark there is a poster on a front yard fence marking the spot where a sixteen-year old couple had been shot dead during a drive by. There was also a vigil of family members mourning in a circle, and they were there when I left and every time I passed after that. It made me paranoid so I skated a little faster through the area every time I came through. I was at the park for only about a half hour before I felt beat. Too much skating in recent weeks had worn my body out and my motivation was gone plus I felt ughhh. The sun was beating down on the park so I found a place in the shade and soon after my body stiffened up and I got cold from the sweat on my shirt and pants. Someone was smoking herb out of a pipe and the aroma traveled over to my nose and made me think of the eight Blueberry plants sunbathing in my backyard. I wanted to get back to try and fight off the caterpillars which were ravaging the plants.

Butterflies and moths innocently flutter around the backyard and land on the plants to lay eggs on the underside of the leaves. If I stare underneath the canopy, I could easily spot them wiggling their way to the buds eager to bore a hole through the center which turns the whole cola brown overnight. These rotted buds didn't go to waste though and if I found them I would dry 'em in the sun to smoke a few hours later or the next day- sometimes with the worm in it. The plants are all only four feet tall, nothing compared to the behemouth plants I heard about up North that had a main cola the size of a man's thigh (according to a friend who worked one of these huge pot farms). I headed down to catch the bus back home and had a few minutes to think before it came. I was psyched to have conjured up the memory of the Skate Rats and a reborn feeling kind of washed over me. It's like drawing from a savings account of good memories. One thing I noticed while riding home is that almost everyone on the bus had a bunch of gear with 'em. Having driven a car for so many years, I was used to tossing everything in the back; but now that I ride the bus more often I see how necessary it is to have a bag.

I caught the middle of a one-way conversation a man was having with his friend that grabbed my attention at the line "I'm used to death." The man, in a sort of mania, was rattling off all the people in his family that had died, commenting that, "cancer sucks the life out of people." He went on to say that he was ready for death and then the conversation became muted and got me thinking about something else. You're forced to listen to each other like you're all a family on the bus.

A homeless man got on and was filthy head to toe. Holding a conversation with himself while he inserted dollars into the machine, he put in about three times the money in fair before rushing to the back, sitting down and folding one leg over the other. Everyone got quiet and began listening to him secretly hoping he would start talking again to relieve the boredom and sluggishness of the bus. For some reason I couldn't stop thinking about the Skate Rats as we again passed E.T. Surf. I began time traveling back to when I'd be riding on the bus from Inglewood in a different direction to arrive in Redondo Beach. It was usually after I got paid from my aquarium job (cash under the table; I was only twelve so I felt rich). I'd hop on the RTD directly across the street from my work to go to E.T. and spend it all, even though it wasn't much. Once I had cash in hand, no matter how little the amount, it began burning a hole in my pocket. E.T.

had that new, epoxy smell from all the surfboards and when I walked in it unconsciously triggered a good feeling in my mind- maybe the glue vapors got me a little high. I'd buy hoodies, like a blue Think Crime sweater that I wore 'til it fell off, or ET Surf sweatpants to be like Chris, who rocked them with a fanny pack. I'd buy one or two things each time like wheels, bolts, grip, rails, shirts, anything skate related. The board wall back then was (and still is) about thirty feet across with some decks covering others, so it took a while to stare at all of them and bug the dude behind the counter to move a few so I could see the graphic underneath. Then I'd roll back to the skate spots in I-Wood, showing off my new shit.

The first time I knew I wanted to skate was when I saw Chris hauling ass down the street in front of my house, the urethane wheels thumping the creases in the sidewalk. I would be transfixed as he pushed mega hard, almost like he couldn't get enough speed. I even payed attention to the way he dressed and wanted to copy his style; it just seemed like the best thing a human could possibly be at that time in history, minus the cigarette smoking. The same goes for skating in general, nothing can take its place and there is no real category for it. It took thousands of years for skating to arrive on earth. Long ago man lived in tribes, threw spears then built up a vast civilization that eventually became perfect for skating. How could there have been a better outcome.

I'd always see Chris with oversized hats and shirts, and socks pulled up past his calves. He was a graffiti artist and always had a marker in his fanny pack for getting up everywhere, in pools, at the bus stop inside Taco Bell, everywhere. The cops beat the shit out of him for it. Nobody ever said it but he was the leader of IWSR and a sort of chronicler for the crew with a memory like an elephant and stories that were epic- some of them lies for sure. We'd gather 'round in a circle behind some mini ramp or the shallow end of a pool to listen after everyone was done skating. The stories he told were always extreme and involved famous skaters, grafitti artists, or any one of the Skate Rats; sometimes he glorified gangbanging, talking about a friend who was a such a hardcore *Blood* that he never used the letter *C* and would say "gimme some bigarettes" right in front of *Crips* in line at the liquor store.

It sucked but sometimes the stories were about people in the area dying. He was the first one to tell us what happened to Norman and Rush. In my neighborhood, shootings and overdoses were common and as I got older these things didn't seem to phase me anymore they became so common. But Norman was different. He was always around us skaters and seemed out of place in the ghetto (just like me). Hanging out at my friend Emielson's we'd always see him coming home from his job at Alpha Beta a half block away. He kinda dressed like a cholo, but just barely so this caused the gang from the adjacent city (Lennox) to view him as a potential target. They got him one night while riding in the rear of a truck after DJing a dance at Inglewood's Jr. High, Crozier. Prowling Lennox gangsters pulled up next to the truck and opened fire on the group of people riding in the flatbed. Norman got hit in the back and died bleeding in the bed of the truck next to a few terrified girls riding beside him. Everything happened so fast that the driver was in shock! He panicked about the police involvement for some unexplained reason and, carrying him with the help of a friend who was riding in the passenger's side, laid him on his porch with a huge hole in his back for his mother to find, then took off.

When I heard about Norman it shook me. Emielson and I would be skating in the street and he'd always approach us with the most positive vibe like we were family. It created such a syntax error in my mind when he was killed because of the simple loss of such pure goodness. Norman was so cool. I knew he would never pass by again so this meant that other people I knew also had the potential of disappearing and it screwed with my head. I had no idea this change had taken place 'cuz it was completely internal. Slowly I turned more despondent towards friends and was reserved about becoming close with anyone, choosing instead to stay remote.

These types of horrible events were so commonplace in the ghetto that kids talked about it like it was nothing- and we hardly ever saw adults around the area and never heard their opinions, let alone conversed with them. The tragic events began mounting one on top of the other when Emielson's brother hung himself in their garage, creating a cursed type of environment on Loma Street. To add to the hard luck of the block, two Jr. members of Inglewood 13 were fucking around with a 22. caliber in a backyard and one accidentally shot himself in the head (according to the one left alive). It was creepy.

My friend Merv also frequented the block. He was never too far away it seemed like, always easily recognizable in the distance rolling up, skating mongol footed. He'd wave me down from up the block as he came close, like "comere", and gave me an update about friends or a heads up on a skate spot- I could see his face now. He was as real as it got and a fixture in our little skate scene. Being older than all of us, nobody ever questioned Merv being around, or dared to, he was just there representing. I never noticed him as any different physically than any of us and just thought everyone had a particular look. Not until he mentioned it himself did I realize his face looked a little funny though, and one day I found out why. He was from a hardcore black neighborhood where insane gangsters ran the block. Somehow he got caught in the middle of some bullshit during a drive by and his head was sprayed with bullets from a Mac 10. He was rushed to the hospital and miraculously saved but in order to remove the bullets they had to slide down part of his face- when they stitched it back up it turned out a little lopsided. It sucks to talk about someone else's tragedy like this and almost seems disrespectful, but it happened.

Merv would skate the mini ramp with everybody and sometimes accompany us to backyard pools and served as a sort of protector and he never hesitated to fight strangers. He smelled funky like someone rejected from there home and unable to properly bathe or get enough to eat- things you take for granted as a kid but become so real as life progresses. But among us he was the strongest cat and displayed a cold reality so vivid words can't get close to the description. What happened to him was unreal. It's crazy having something so devastating told to you and trying to understand it at such a young age. I could only imagine it through my filter, but really I had no clue how insane it was. We were all products of the ghetto.

Being around influential skaters like IWSR helped to lift me out of the poverty mind state I was in, and made me see further. Chris lived closest to me and had to skate up my street to get home from school or his girlfriend's house so I'd see him all the time, only he never stopped. Sometimes he'd be out skating or talking to Little George or driving by in Big George's station wagon that was completely covered in stickers. He was the first dude I ever knew that ground his Indys to the axle.

Other times on my way to the Psycho Bowl on La Cienega, I would run into him coming home from private school without his board and he'd be styled out in fresh Nikes and matching clothes, waiting at the crosswalk with both hands on the straps of his backpack; you could see who some of the other Skate Rats got their style from. An original. He would carve his own boards out of rectangular Zplanks that had all the concave of a regular board, ready to customize- just one of the realest skaters I've ever known.

Music was really important to him and I heard he later became a DJ on Loyola Marymount's *KXLU*. Once I skated all the way to Westchester with him so he could get the new *GWAR* cd the day it came out. He was also into Hip Hop and wore a *Public Enemy* hat with *Huero* tagged on the side. *Huero* was spray painted and tagged everywhere at skate spots in Inglewood along with the rest of the skate rats under *IWSR* like a roll call. Years before Chris, Mondo and a few other Skate Rats were famous for ripping off the *Dogtown* factory and flooding the streets of Inglewood with Eric Dressen, Aaron Murray and Scott Oster decks. Rumor was they took pictures posing in a bedroom after the heist with wall to wall boards in the background and for years after you would see Dogtown decks everywhere in the neighborhood. I never got a hold of one.

My first board was a Vision Gator (Mark Ragowski [Gator] was later the subject of a documentary I saw in theatres when it came out. He went crazy in the late-eighties, raping and killing his girlfriend's best friend, receiving life in prison). I got the board from my brother who, in an idiotic moment, decided one day he was going to test a skateboard out in front of a shop by riding it up and down the street- somehow without the employees noticing- and ended up having to buy the complete. He was bitter about the purchase 'cuz he was forced to and just ended up locking it in his room. One day when his car broke down I went with him to try and start it a few blocks up and he rode his new complete and I rode my bike.

While he was making the car worse by trying to fix it, I rode the board up a large driveway embankment and immediately felt a connection. It created the best sensation in my legs and I really felt what it was like to ride a professional board. The set up had the old Thunders with the reptile on the base plate and Vision Blur wheels. When we were done I nagged and nagged and somehow convinced my brother to let me buy it off of him. He didn't even ride the thing and saw how bad I wanted it so he agreed to sell it to me in a moment of compassion, but wouldn't shut up about the money for years to come, still claiming I owe him a few bucks. The board was the classic neon vortex that Vision reprints retro graphics of today, sans Ragoswki's name. It had a skid plate and nose guard that I took off when I started learning tricks and carving pools. It was a world away from my swap meet board. The wood was stained dark blue and the grip tape was cut to show the Vision logo on the front.

I've found myself spending hours thinking about how lucky I was to have started skating and stuck with it, and that it's not just something I did when I was a kid. The gnarly injuries and hard work seem justified when I think about it like that, other times my ankle gives out or my back seizes up and I second guess it. Some people in my life think it's childish for me to skate anyways because I have major responsibilities. Skateboarding just isn't real to them. The only people who approve are my kids, because they haven't formed a bias yet and they get happy when dad flips his board.

Looking down at my deck as I ride and hustle to get a few miles down the road I feel a little jaded and being that my wife moved out taking the car and kids with her, I am using my board for transportation. Who wouldn't leave- I'm a fucking idiot. Growing weed and chasing a skateboarding dream; both costing money and time that's not coming back. I'm a little thrown off by the sudden downturn of luck and am actually writing this to keep the depression a safe distance away. I realized that all the skating over the years had taken it's toll on my body; and pushing through crumbling asphault makes it worse but I can't stop to complain or even to walk or look around at the cars everywhere in every direction blaring their headlights in my face. The city looks a hundred percent more shitty if you're hungry and depressed and me right now; at these times skating seems silly to me too. I just have to keep pushing down the street with the last of my strength- to make a few more feet of progress between the voids and get home. The urge to stop and stare for infinity (at the very least) and take in what's happening almost overwhelms me, but like a scared animal I keep hurrying back to safety. I feel like my past is chasing me so to keep it at bay a jolt of energy comes from deep inside and before I know it several blocks go by. My shirt collar was covering my face but I couldn't stand the smell of my breath so I dropped it and pressed the button for the light. I looked at a Peterbuilt semi rolling past, the street lights bouncing off the chrome rims and the glossed door panels. It's hook up cables bounced in the back as it inched up to turn and head onto the 110. I couldn't help but think of my pop who used to shine the rims of trucks for a living in San Bernadino; and I thought it was a sign, like his ghost encouraging me to keep moving. My fatigue humbled me and I suddenly felt sorry for my Dad and thought of the despair he must've felt being illiterate and stuck in a world where everything seemed against the guy. As the truck rolled by I found myself trying to understand him, and put my suffering aside for a moment as almost trivial. He made a terrible living walking around truck stops asking semi drivers at rest if they'd like him to shine their trucks. Most drivers just shook their heads no, or to be nice sometimes said 'maybe later'. Now that I'm older I can really understand the depression that comes on when you're forced into a corner and at the mercy of other people for your living.

Several times as a kid I went to stay with him in a trailer park where he lived in an old, gutted school bus. In my opinion it was a step up from the desolate petting zoo he lived at before, where acres and acres of empty cages overgrown with weeds and spider webs awaited a mythical reopening date. The bus was the classic yellow with black and stuck out among the trailers in the park. It was about a hundred yards from a river and behind was a drought-ridden forest that went for miles, making the trailer park road the doorway to civilization with a quick escape route into a lawless territory at my Dad's back (the kind of situation he preferred).

I was already at the age where I had caught the skating bug and I brought my board with me everywhere. When I visited I'd divide my time between fishing in the river and skating miniature full pipes abandoned by the state for use in an underground water system. Dozens of them were lined up in rows behind my Dad's trailer. The concrete pipes were only about seven feet tall at best and were a super tight fit that only allowed for quick fakie pumps and a few hurried backside carves. A friend I met that lived about a half mile up the way had a dilapidated mini ramp that caught me off guard and sent me to the bottom on my face too many times to count. The ramp looked like a child made it and was on its last legs. The one time I skated it pretty much did it in for good. It seemed weird to me because in my city where there's a construction site on every corner that left everything unlocked after hours, ramps were *way* easier to re-ply. My buddy didn't seem to think anything was wrong with it and went about doing boneless tricks, lay back grinds and a few early grabs. With so many bunk skate spots, fishing seemed like the better option so I passed the time most days walking up and down the river trying to catch trout and getting lost looking at strange swimming beetles and water skeeters; following darting shadows, skipping across fungus covered boulders and falling on my ass and bouncing into the water frequently.

My dad had explored the forest behind the trailer park thoroughly, so one day when I was staying with him he got motivated and took me for a hike into the mountains that lasted for hours. We started early in the morning and followed a stream deep into a valley that was part of the San Bernadino Mountain Range. There were pools all over and trails that went forever into the dusty hills. As we hiked a thick silence that never broke rang in my ears and we went almost the entire time not talking as my dad stayed mostly in his head. He brought a pellet gun that he tucked in his waste and a shotgun that he always held with the stock open for safety, both guns were for shooting at birds and squirrels we saw on the trail- at least the trail he had in mind. My Dad went anywhere he wanted.

Using the pellet gun, he blew the brains out of a sun bathing lizard and splashed blood all over a huge boulder, freaking me out. We walked off and left it shaking in place as it died cooking in the July sun. I didn't think it was cool but had no voice at that age so I said nothing as he continued along taking pot shots at birds and darting rabbits. When he wasn't shooting, the silence returned and all that I heard was the wind rustling through the air and beetles making a high pitched buzz in the dry grass. Then he'd blast his shotgun and all hell would break loose. Birds would flock out of the trees with all the other critters running for their lives, and it almost seemed like the forest shed leaves in every direction because of the noise. I remember seeing a squirrel suddenly light up red as he ran with buckshot planted in his behind then disappear into a hole to die. It sucked.

The smell of pine floated through the air and the California sun beat down on us and cooked the trails, so we stopped at shaded pools for long periods to beat it. There were a few here and there along the stream we followed. We said nothing to each other, like early homonids valuing speech very little and resonating more with nature and the deafening quiet. I'd throw my fishing line into promising looking pools- some super clear with rock lining the bottom and crevices that ran deep into the granite face, some of them with small waterfalls- but caught nothing on the entire hike. We walked so much my legs were burning, and it didn't make sense to me but I know now why we kept going to the point of exhaustion. It was my Dad's way of escaping. He was trying to hike beyond the hand he was dealt in life and ascend above an overly complicated world to a life where everything was clear and simple. To him only nature made sense. As long as he had a loaded shotgun and something to shoot at (and a carton of

Marlboros), he was straight. If the forests around were more fruitful he might not have ever come back and would've gladly stayed and lived off the land and escaped the identity smacked on him by society, grazing on the mulch of creation. Later when we got home we feasted on a meal of potato salad and fried chicken continuing the mutual silence we had maintained the entire day. I was almost dehydrated and hardly had strength to eat; but it was nothin' for my pop who'd been in the wild since he was a kid, his face always a dark shade of red from sun exposure. Next time he said we'd take tents and food to a site deeper near a river. But it was always next time.

When he was gone working I'd hike on my own up and down the river, mostly to avoid my step mom. There were sections of it with no bank where trees had taken over creating a canopy above the running water. In between the trees I'd find a small opening and try to cast without hooking the branches, breaking the surface of the calm waters where dozens of circles formed continuously from trout snatching insects. It was easier to get around walking down the middle of the river where it was shallow- I found more fish this way. Once I came upon a butt naked couple having sex up against a tree. They quickly stopped when they heard my feet splashing and the man put his junk away and pretended to play it off while the lady was confused and asked what was wrong. He mumbled something to her about a kid and I just trudged by like I didn't see anything.

Some parts of the river were loaded with fish and the only problem was keeping hooks from snagging and snapping off. If I lost too many that meant no more fishing. When there were a lot of trout I'd be so excited to tie on my rig that I'd prick myself with the hooks, and time would slow down making it feel like an eternity went by before I was ready to cast. The sound of the water flowing excited something primal inside me, making me rush and drop my hooks and tangle the line. Here and there were houses hidden in the trees along the road and some were right next to the river. Once someone's pet cat stood by innocently watching as I fished and I didn't think anything of it. She stood there licking her paws and even winked her eyes at me when I looked at her. The kitty didn't come too close 'til I caught a fish and quickly brought it onto the ground before I lost it. As soon as it hit the ground and started flopping in the dirt the cat leaped toward me, savagely snatched it and ran off with the fish in it's mouth, breaking the line and making away with my last hook. I ran after him but he darted under a house through a cubby hole.

Kneeling, I watched his silhouette holding down the fish and taking bites as it flopped in the dirt. I thought of every way I could to somehow get the hook back, I even knocked on the front door and explained but the lady just looked at me like I was speaking another language, so I had to leave it.

During the week I went with my Dad to the local truck stop in Ontario where he would shine rigs in the 100 plus degree heat. It would be so intense my feet made indentations in the asphault. We walked around row after row of semis as he tried to make deals with the drivers to shine their rims. While he talked I would look at the insects that had collected on the semis grill from all over the U.S. Butterflies and moths were frozen in place along with dragonflies and huge beetles that cracked and disintegrated when I tried to pull them off. Sometimes my sister would be with us and she and

I would escape the heat by standing underneath the tall trailers watching my dad bust his ass buffing out the chrome rims and blackening his skin in the sun. It was no place for kids.

His stocky frame would never let up as he went from wheel to wheel making his living with filthy rags that brought out a piercing, mirrored shine. When he made enough money to buy groceries and gas *(if* he did) we'd head back to the trailer park and as soon as we reached the bus I'd take off on my skate. There was nothing but white trash all around the place. It was the kind of area where you'd see a momma cat and her litter abandoned in a box next to other belongings on the side of the road; the majority of the people had no teeth either and everyone was broke. It was a little canyon that the rest of the world forgot and looked so desolate that people driving by stepped hard on the gas pedal when they saw it.

I quickly got homesick and started to panic. I couldn't skate and I didn't know anyone. My anxiety peeked when my dad said he worked it out with my mom and we were going to stay another month. Like a brat I called her practically crying and begged her to come up and get me but she didn't care and called me a big baby for complaining. I kept begging and finally she gave in after calling me a shithead and everything else, then got on the phone and convinced my dad to drive me back to Inglewood. All I could think about was skating and not the trouble my dad would have to go through dropping me off because he was broke as a joke and it was a ton of gas to take me home. What a dick. But I was just a kid and that whole trip was weird for me, and I guess I wanted my momma.

Once I got back I went on a skate rampage and dropped by all my friend's houses to get some long overdue skating in. I was so full of energy I skated across the entire city 'til I was exhausted and learned tricks I didn't think I could ever do. It's a true addiction, and like opium, once the habit has begun it has to be maintained for life.

George and Shorty asked me where I had been for so long but I just laughed and kept on skating. We would all just randomly show up at the bank to chain in Ladera Heights; it was a weird, psychic thing, we'd all just go there at the same time, even if none of us had been in a few days. There was also a sharp metal ledge near it that we always hit up on the way in that I did fifties and backside nosegrinds that cut thick gouges in my Indys. I can't remember even learning them, and the same goes for 360 flips, I just knew how to do them- that was it (a gift from skateboarding). Both spots weren't a bust so we spent a lot of time on 'em, sometimes just using the ledge to stall nosepicks on; or the bank to chain doing frontside and backside ollies like a quarter pipe. Shorty would always bag on the way I did method grabs over the chain, calling them stinkbug 'cuz of how stiff my legs and the grab were. Because I had been at my dad's and off my board for so long it was like skating was new to me. The funny thing is that while I was away my mind kept developing and it felt like I was now better. I was with my two mentors as well, one older and the other younger so I started to flow with the day and into the night, losing track of time in a skate mania.

I learned to get places faster and to push with both feet from Shorty who I watched do it on long trips, when we only had a vague destination in mind. More than trying to get somewhere, we mostly stop at spots along the way to get some skating in, and sometimes this constituted the whole skate trip. Some of the most memorable sessions with Shorty and George happened when we were just waiting some place for someone to meet us or some contest to start, or just for the bus to come. George wouldn't take any obstacle for granted. He'd use cracks in the pavement to boost large Chinese ollies and then G-Turn someone's driveway afterward. He always repeated tricks over and over again, nailing them perfectly every time. I could never pinpoint Shorty's style because he'd do such a variety of moves- I tried hard to figure out what he was thinking but never could. He'd go from skating a mini ramp to doing kickflip foot plants on the end of a ledge, or fakie big spins (mamma jammas) that would float to axle stall on a curb. And we had no cameras, no internet, just our mentals to record the good times.

It was around 1989 and people rode bigger wheels, and Bullet 66mms were popular along with skinny rails and pizza grip (really coarse grip tape). A lot of people road them 'til they were 40mm or less and I remember seeing dudes with them smaller than that busting crazy tricks, not thrown off by the wheel size whatsoever. They rode them the same whether they were new or right next to the bearing. Hardcore skaters who just rolled out of their houses to any viable spot with a vague image in their mental about what tricks to do and just an urge from the universe to bless it up. The originators; self-motivated, making it up as they went along.

Shorty and George always had new wheels and decks with stickers overlapping each other across the graphic and between the grip tape on the front, repeating Santa Monica Airlines stickers or Rocco Think Crime ones. They both had that glimmering smile across their face that came (I assumed) from being sponsored and they never seemed to lose their energy, fueled only by Cheetos, Twinkies and grape soda. A lot of times we skated around 'til the sun grew huge and began dropping down behind the buildings like they were mountains and melting the city. When it got dark we'd skate under the light posts like moths gathering around the glow and never stop to see what time it was, nor were any of us expected back or even missed.

That was when I was a little shit and indestructible, now the soreness I feel after long skates makes me realize that at 37, all that skating had taken it's toll on my body, and pushing through crumbling asphault at night with a wet shirt makes that feel more real. It's like déjà vu. I push to my house from the bus stop using both legs, switching up when one gets tired, something Shorty used to do. If our bodies are a prison for our soul, then skating allows for a little more lift and freedom of movement. I have to stop myself from daydreaming so I don't miss my stop, which is hard 'cuz all I can think about lately is growing up around the Skate Rats. It's almost like a memory relapse where I'm now just seeing the value of that beautiful experience. I hold my board in front of me and spin the wheel with my finger, thinking way back to when I took the bus with Shorty to Skip Englomb's house (the founder of Santa Monica Airlines)- an all day trip. I went over all the steps to try and relive them. I remember being barely just teenagers transferring from bus to bus all the way to Inglewood we skated into a Santa Monica neighborhood to his house. He was psyched to see us when we got there and showed us a deck he had halfway carved for Julian Stranger out of a plank of wood, like a caveman inventing the first skateboard. As a youngster I didn't understand how spiritual that was, but now looking back, it seems like the coolest way a board could possibly be constructed.

Recently I saw Skip in the Z-boys documentary and it tripped me out, and I especially knew it would trip Shorty out to hear about him. Skip's name comes up all the time in talk about skate history (especially when it comes to Natas). I remember him smiling and doting on Shorty as we'd hang around Rip City where he'd pick up money and a complete for any number of trips, or just for nothing because Skip gave him anything he wanted. Once we stopped by the shop to get pads or clothes or something before a mini-ramp contest on the beach in Santa Monica that he and George dragged me along to. It was a mission to get there by bus but worth it because everybody in the industry showed up. We saw the Gonz destroy the ramp on a long board wearing a Pro-tec helmet with ear protectors. He went forever without bailing, busting huge frontside ollies that floated slow motion in the air, and the coolest fast plants to fakie and bonelesses. Frankie Hill was there and did a huge kickflip to fakie on the ramp (way ahead of his time). He was my favorite from the Powell videos and I remember thinking that I wanted to be him when he rolled up with his knee pads tucked under his arms and a brand new set-up, smiling huge as everyone said what's up to him.

Shorty could hardly get any practice because it was a gnarly snake session and he ended up not making the cut. It didn't matter how he placed because Skip really liked him and knew the nature of skating- anyways M. Payne could do no wrong. Once at a different contest at the Santa Monica Boys Club I saw Skip watch George and Shorty's practice like a true fan of the sport, observing quietly with his arms folded and a serious look on his face, not unlike pro baseball and basketball scouts or coaches sizing up the new season's picks. But rather than observing to choose the best new am he seemed to truly dig the evolution of the sport and the innovation taking place right in front of him. Skip had solid riders, always. The team was multi-generation and sometimes the young dudes would be packed in the car with the older dudes, so Shorty had stories about Alan Peterson destroying a contest, describing tricks to us that seemed unreal.

George remembered sitting next to Jeff Hartzel in a car on the way to a contest and said his dreadlocks reeked like crazy and kept rubbing all over his face. Skating's gnarly.

George was getting SMA boards by then and Skip was really interested in his skating. Shorty kept telling him to get on SMA as his Jesse Martinez/World Industries connect was unreliable. Skip dealt with his riders one on one and hooked them up with a healthy amount of gear. He'd give Shorty money just to give him money. Sometimes it was to travel and visit other team members, like the time he sent him to SF where he skated with Natas and Jim Thiebaud. We all knew that he was going to S.F. because he had been telling us about it for like a week. When he got back he showed up with some sick mid-top suede vans and we all wanted to know about the trip so after skating he talked about it while we all sat on our boards in a circle. He said Natas was doing switch 180s over sewer grates, which took him a while to describe as we hardly even nollied back then or even skated switch (our noses weren't even that big). I vividly remember him talking about hauling ass with Natas and Jim somewhere in SF as he watched Natas cruise up to a rail and say "watch this Jim", and then 180 nose grind it, which Shorty described instead of naming because the trick hadn't been invented yet.

The next day I tried switch 180s in front of my house for hours and hours 'til I could do them. The best feeling was showing George the move first try while we were skating to a spot just after that. After I did it he laughed, then I started laughing.

Most people at the bus stop I'm at are on their phones, talking or listening to music. My phone bill is overdue so all I could do besides staring at the river of cars is think. When I got on the bus I zoned out and began to admire the curving stretches of road. It sounds abstract but I started to realize that humans enjoy taking the curve (like the Golden Spiral) more than trying to maintain a straight line. I thought about the contrast between the bus and the Metro trains here in L.A. as I stared out the window. The Metro trains are more visually stimulating because they take you in between freeways and underground, then on to huge depots like Union Station in downtown all at a high rate of speed which feels both sophisticated and dangerous at the same time. There's a whole different culture riding the trains that's invisible to the world, like the bus, the people dependent on it are mainly the underclass. Thousands of riders pack the platforms waiting for them- some transferring train to train or from buses to the train, and vice versa. At certain stops (because of the delay when the doors are open) vendors get on and walk up and down the isles trying to sell candy, chips, sodas, gum and blunt wraps. I thought about how universal this was down through history. Wherever a stream of people is consistent there will always be somebody setting up shop to sell them something when they pass.

One day when I was riding the Metro back from Silverlake a blind man got on in Watts and stood center stage by the door asking for change from everyone in a joking way; he mixed his words with broken Spanish and English starting with "ladies and gentlemen, signors and signoritas..." He was pushing 70 and had on the most filthy, raggedy clothes. I was curious as to how he became blind so I asked him (not even raising my voice because I knew he had a heightened sense of hearing) and he immediately spotted where it came from and looking right at me he said, while pointing at the back of his head, "I got shot!" He paused for a second afterwards like he was thinking back to the incident. Before I asked him this I saw a few people contemplating giving him money- some ladies rummaging in their purses and a few guys looking in their wallets and then closing them- but just after he answered me a whole slew of riders began bringing money up to him or handing it to other people walking up who pressed it to his hand. It was at least ten dollars altogether, which he started stuffing in the lining of his boxers somewhere by his butt. I'm guessing he put it there because other homeless people picked his pockets. He got off at the next stop and thanked everyone for helping. This would've never happened on the bus because the driver wouldn't allow it, but the Metro trains are different, the driver is nowhere to be seen.

After linking up with two different trains without a ticket I got off at my stop just in front of L.A.X. at about 10 p.m. and walked two miles to a bus stop, waiting thirty minutes for one. Before it came I stared at the full moon, which looked as big as the sun, and thought about our galaxy and about Earth's position on the outer arms far away from the super-massive black hole at the center. A lot to imagine with maybe 18 stars visible. What if life is seeded on the outer edges of the galaxy (in the cut), like where we are; a civilization could develop for millions, maybe billions or trillions of years undetected. That made me think about how many times skateboarding was developed on other planets by other people and how it could be as ancient as the universe- or maybe it's native to California and never before seen in the universe, ever. Not with this much steeze anyways.

3

My brain's hard drive is stuffed to the gills with memories of the craziness in the city- stuff most people don't see 'cuz they aren't looking for abandoned skate spots. Traveling on freeways in LA, running from gangsters, being in the darkest creepiest spots in the city late at night on my board, not knowing how I got there; feeling vulnerable and my only choice is to skate faster and hope my mind gets distracted. Even then I have a hard time staying with the reality I'm in. Feeling the concrete and ollieing up curbs that look exactly like the last few thousand I ollied up. I'm completely burnt on the present. Right now I'm tripping out on writing this book and looking back to when I was a kid and just started skating is one of my only pure comforts, aside from skating itself; but even then I find myself holding back because my gear is so busted. My shoes are falling apart and I skate mostly switch, because skating for transportation I use my tail more to get up curbs and ruin that side of the board and shoe more than the other- whatever.

When I was a kid I put duct tape all over the front of my shoe when they wore out from ollieing so much and sometimes even wrapped my socks with it. I had sweat rings around my hats that dried into white patches; and I remember having unlimited energy to skate and learn tricks, so much that I was never home. I just pushed around anywhere, trying to link up with friends and skate something. I was always thinking about the future, wondering how long it would be 'til I could do a McTwist or what my pro board would look like. It gets me psyched to get back there in my head when I had that much hope, no responsibilities and all I did was stare at ripped up Transworld Magazines over and over with bubbling pages from getting wet in the bathroom, and all of them missing their covers and then some. On days I'd stay home from school I would read every word on every page again and again, even the lists of product on the mail order ads, envisioning the perfect set up. I'd memorize all the pros names: Gator, Mike Vallely, Jason Jesse, the brothers Steve and Mickey Alba, Tony Magnusson, Ron Allen, Omar Hassan, Natas, Rob Roskopp, Hosoi, Ken Park, Neil Blender, Marty 'Jinx' Jimenez, Corey Obrien, Mark Gonzales, Blaze Blouin, Steve Caballero, Chris Miller, Steve

Steadham, Mike McGill, Lance Mountain, Jeff Kendall, Eric Dressen, Tommy Geurrero, Julien Stranger, Ed Templeton and on and on.

My whole life back then was consumed by skating. With a phenomenon in my neighborhood like George, it was almost inevitable that I pursued it. The blueprint was right in front of me. Seeing live how far he pushed the envelope is what set the standard so high in my mind. He was *so* clean. Watching him skate made me forget about any other ambition I had, save for skating. He wasn't an offering for the whole world to see because he never turned pro, but for anyone that knows about him and was around when he was skating, you might as well have been watching the best video part up to that time. It was like skateboarding was expressing its new evolution through him. Riding with his hat backwards and arms extended symmetrically, tricks would just peel off like butter and anything he couldn't do or invent another Skate Rat had covered; the crew always sticks in my mind as the cleanest vision of skating in the late eighties.

George and Shorty would always pick me up to go on trips. We'd mostly take the bus and push long distances in between. Everywhere we went they would find something to skate. It seems like they'd come up with the newest tricks spontaneously out of the creative field and whether we skated a mini-ramp, vert or street all the new shit would go down. Once they brought me with them to skate the Culver City vert ramp (the one in *Rubbish Heap*) and I watched George come out of nowhere with tricks he obviously had been doing for a while but were new to me- it was like I was watching a seasoned pro. Backside airs, frontside nose-bones, smith grinds. The ramp was only 10 or 11 feet high but it seemed like we were on top of a mountain, and the only noise I heard was the wind and the sound of wheels on the wood ramp.

He was like a Babe Ruth of skating; a seemingly common person that just masters the sport, savant-like, and becomes a phenomenon. I was blown away that day watching George catch the highest airs and stick his little foot out judo and anti-judo almost in slow motion. It was sick to see his hand waiting for the board on backside late grabs or tweaked stalefish as his wheels bounced off the coping making that metal sound from the slightly loose clamps. On backside airs he let his back foot lean and curl the board like Eric D. I was in awe because I could only do a backside air sometimes and even then my foot would come off the board, and not on purpose, but nothing like George's ollies or leans to tale. I almost expected him to do a Mctwist.

I saw Eric D there once smoking a joint with Scott Oster and the boys on and old sofa against the wall bragging that he could blunt fakie the vert ramp, which everyone was calling bullshit on causing him to get up and try it until the sun went down. Eric Dressen was probably the best skater in LA at that time. I'd always see him at the Transitions miniramp in downtown just shredding- frontside noseblunt slides to tail grab in, front salads across the length of the deck, gigantic ollies, everything; I would just watch with my jaw dropped. When I recently saw his Santa Cruz *V-Day* part (a sort of video documentary) it brought back all those old feelings that buzzed in me as a kid seeing him skate. It was beyond what any words could describe. To me Eric D was more than a movie-star. The old school Thrasher photos in *V-Day* of him kneeling with his Dogtown board and wearing shades (his hair hanging down *new wave* style), and especially the flick of the tweaked method out of the quarter pipe on the boardwalk, triggered the craziest high in me.

He was a Venice local. Skating there back then was so fresh and influential to me mainly because of those guys. It was only two busses away if I skated to the LAX transit terminal a few miles from my house and as a kid I never ran out of the energy to push there. My absence would go unnoticed by my mom and usually it would be after dark when I got back. I would always see Jeff Hartzel cruising around the boardwalk with Joey Tran, Tuma, Little Man, Daniel Castillo, Jesse Martinez, Tim Jackson (who would be climbing the Venice wall with endless grabbing wallride tricks), Butch Sturbins,

Dressen- all the classic Venice heads. Once skating a contest by the wall I lost my board during a run and it shot over to Jesse Martinez who deftly caught it and shot it back to me, all while kneeling like a cholo. The boardwalk was where all the pros hung out. There wasn't hardly any filming done back then so most skating was something you could only see in person. Sponsors picked dudes up based on contests; 'cuz that's just where they were. Videos were scarce and when I finally saw H-Streets *Shackle Me Not*, it was already a few years old.

A while later I met Dressen through Scott Oster. I tagged along a few times while they were filming for the OJs video *Streets of Fire* at the famous bank to chain in Ladera Heights. I knew Oster from skating there and he'd always let me tag along on missions; once it was with Eric D to charge some skate some spots in the area around L.A.X. We rolled around out front of Scott's house trying tricks for more than an hour waiting for him, and Scott kept complaining about how late Eric was. When he finally showed up the excuse given for his tardiness was that he 'had to hump.' We drove to the empty Westchester Park pool (that I still session) in Scott's jeep and passed around the new Thrasher Magazine to get pumped before we got out to skate. Eric was riding his just released Everslick Santa Cruz (his was a prototype) and I was drooling over the set-up. We jumped the fence and started skating the square pool that dips to a deep point in the middle making banks. He went at it and was like a powerhouse just destroying the pool, doing almost head high big spin tail grabs out of the steep bank, pop shuv-its, 360s, everything. I saw him take advantage of every hit, busting all the new shit with no camera around and just Scott and I watching. He did a caveman on the short rail dropping into the deep end of the pool but bailed it too many times and just moved on. It's no wonder skaters in the area I knew were so good- these were the pros they grew up seeing.

Dressen and all the Venice skaters knew who George was and for years people would tell me stories about him, like when he and Guy Mariano battled it out to the end at contests. I heard this from other Skate Rats because George never talked about himself. Only once did I hear him say something about a trick and that was after he stopped skating (referring to a pressure flip, saying in a matter of fact way that it would take him two days to learn it). Way before he quit I remember lurking in my neighborhood skating around the arcing street Chris lived on and suddenly seeing George 360 backside grabbing off a jump ramp in the middle of the road. He did it right as I turned the corner, grabbing late as he tapped his tail on the lip and launched out spinning perfectly, landing exactly straight after the rotation. Again and again he repeated it going bigger every time. I got so psyched that I tried to skate it too because my instincts said go! I had never seen a video in my life, but seeing George skate blew anything like that away- it was the genuine artifact. When I did see videos I thought to myself that he was destined to be in them and that it was just a matter of time before his part showed everyone how to really skate; the same way genius musicians are able to interpret centuries old music and show modern conductors how it was really meant to be played. I'd go with him to demos and contests watching him do all his tricks off the highest jump ramps, busting flatground in between and skating with pros and ams that had the most respect for him, always asking him "where the fuck you been at!"

He would tweak methods and casually let his feet curl upward as he seemed to swim through the air without even trying, landing with very little impact. On mini ramps he mastered the chink-chink and would 50-50 to revert all day, do the highest frontside stailfishs and all the blunts and smith grinds. The more I was around, the more tricks I saw him do. He had something for everything. If he would've kept skating who knows how far he would've got- but we're on a different timeline now.

He always skated the school across from Chris' house where the Inglewood Stoners brought their jump ramp on Friday when school got out and just left it all weekend for anyone to skate. The foundation on the side of the classroom trailers was wood and slanted. Like nothing George would do arcing frontside wallrides, putting his hand on the wall; crailsnatchers and long backside wallrides. He really rode the wall too, compressing with it like a surfer in a barrel, in no hurry to land. Little George was the best. Once in a different part of town he just showed up out of the blue to a quarter pipe me and some other bozos were skating in the street. He turned off his course to hit it like a patrolling reef shark and launched out at least three feet to a backside disaster, immediately bringing it out of hang up, then circled a few times repeating the same trick (every one getting bigger); after the last one he just vanished into the streets.

His place was behind a row of two car garages (that people lived in), which had an opening between them leading to his apartment. It was facing a courtyard lined with hydrangea that hardly ever survived blooming without getting whacked to pieces by some kid. His older sister raised him herself with no parents and spoiled the crap out of him. He lived way closer to Manchester than me, which cut Inglewood in half, and right near Mr. J's burgers (a landmark and gang hangout where a friend of mine was killed). Everyone in the neighborhood ate at the place, but mostly there'd be cholos with Nike Cortez shoes on, shaved heads and creased Dickies filling the stalls. Mr. J. didn't care if you were a gangster or a snot nosed little whiteboy, he wouldn't let anyone go without talking to them and asking about relatives and friends, what they did that day, the weather-anything. Then he'd hand over the chili cheeseburgers and oversized onion rings that were so greasy they fell through the bag.

I had witnessed a friend of a friend hock the fattest lugi onto a tray at Mr. J's, then suck it up with a ketchup bottle- looking up at me as he did it with almost no expression on his face. After that I wouldn't use the bottles. The same guy would get the biggest thrill out of throwing a brick through a car window. There were some weird people in the ghetto. Once after a long skate day a bunch of us were eating outside Mr. J's when Shorty took a ketchup bottle and pretended to ejaculate as he squirted ketchup onto the floor, moaning in a drawn out scene, making everyone laugh.

When I first moved to the neighborhood and was learning where everything was, I rode a bike all over and was hit by cars more than once, my body putting a mean dent in one of them. I just explored everywhere not knowing which areas to stick to and which ones to avoid. Riding near George's house I was approached a bunch of times by a guy named Memo, (a young gangster I later became friends with), who caught up to me on his bike asking me where I was from. It was almost like he was patrolling the block the way he'd ride up and down the street, always appearing day or night anytime I came through. He'd ride parallel with me and say "where you from foo?" I would say over and over, Inglewood, thinking he meant literally where I was from and not what gang. This went on for a while with me insisting over and over that I was from Inglewood, and after seeing how stupid I was he would just give up and ride away. A few years later working as paperboys together Memo and I were chased by Lennox gang members on the road, which seemed like fun to him but scared the shit out of me. We were packed with other paperboys in our boss-lady's car on the way back from a Daily Breeze night out at an arcade or something like that. When these youngsters (who were watching us the whole night) were harassing us on the road, driving right next to us, I freaked out and kept ducking saying they were going to kill us while Memo threw up gang signs at them, laughing the whole time! The boss lady seemed to think it was hilarious as well.

This wasn't the only thing that happened when it came to Lennox prowling my neighborhood. I remember pounding on a neighbor's doors to let me in after being chased by them one night on the way home from a friends and hiding under a car, then being spotted and forced to keep running. I was let in and saved by people down the street who almost had a heart attack from me banging so hard on the door, just narrowly escaping some anonymous gangsters in a Regal with tinted windows who were out to kill someone. Around where I lived it was crazy like that.

4

Growing up my family was on welfare with seven kids in our house. My mom, who did it all by herself, was always urging me to work at an early age. I was on the lookout for a source of money and being a paperboy was super tough because none of the people I delivered to ever paid their bill. I'd return at night to collect, try to catch them on the weekend- nothing. I couldn't get paid. A friend of mine that hung out with the Skate Rats said that he was quitting a job helping at the Tropical Fish store nearby and I should go take his place. I took his advice and went in to talk to the owner who said that was o.k. Soon after I began a life of perpetual smelly fish hands. I was paid under the table forty dollars per week for helping out two days after school and on Saturdays. The address was 720 and I always thought of Tony Hawk when I went in and saw the numbers above the door. There were huge grafitti pieces visible on the roof that ran forever, like they were commissioned by the city. It was next to a meat market that had the best aroma coming out of the vents; the scent would cause me to follow it like a cartoon character floating through the air, being pulled by the smell to buy a mustard burger, a hot dog, whatever- it was all good.

I cleaned gnarly-stinky tanks, packed up feeder goldfish for regulars to give their huge Oscars and did other chores like sweeping up the place, or fetching live Brine Shrimp. Some customers owned giant Arrowanas or huge Pacu (the toothless cousin of the Piranha) that they crammed into large tanks. The resident Arowana in our shop was almost three feet long and swam back and forth like it was pacing, it's huge scales shimmering in the cramped tank. I did just about every task in the shop that a twelve-year old couldn't screw up. He was a stocky dude that swished his sandals around the store, refusing to pick up his feet when he walked. Sometimes he'd bring his dad who spoke no English and when I talked to him he just laughed liked the Buddha and nodded his head 'til I left. Metal encased electric cables ran all over the store and more than a few times I was given a quick jolt and got fuckin' shocked when accidentally touching the wrong part with wet, fishy hands.

When it was slow I would zone out in the back of the store looking at all the crazy colored tropical and saltwater fish, like the Cobalt Blue Discus. They're shaped kind of like an Angel Fish: they're barely a line when you see 'em dead on (like a disc) with the craziest blue and turquoise stripes painted on them. They were fed tiny, live tubefix worms that smelled like dog shit and were sold by the scoop to customers that wanted to treat their fish. I got bit by some of the crazy-aggressive saltwater trigger fish and stayed way away from the poison ones. The colors on some fish was so vivid under the fluorescent lighting it almost looked supernatural. I miss that.

When I got paid from the aquarium I'd go right across the street to the bus stop without stopping home and head to E.T. Surf to buy skate gear. My Korean boss didn't pay me shit, but I couldn't get cash anywhere from anyone in my life but Bruce. It was money under the table and was more than I ever made from my paper route. Skating was always what I wanted to do ever since I could remember, but because my home situation was unstable I had to have a whole string of jobs that eventually interrupted my progression out of first place.

Before I started working full time and it took over my life, there was a brief period where I didn't work at all and I wished that'd stayed permanent but it didn't. I was in tenth grade and was missing a lot of school going away on skating trips to San Diego with Mark Partain (who headed my board sponsor, Renegade) and we'd stay at his partner Glenn's house. The company was small but had a good concept- weed and skating- and was backed by the clothing company Bronze Age. They printed zig zag rolling paper shirts with their logo on it that everyone would get psyched to see me in, but whose meaning I was oblivious to. I would just smile and say 'cool' when other skaters would smile big and tell me how cool my shirt was, thinking I smoked ganja. I didn't until I was twenty-two.

My mom would have to write lengthy excuse notes for my teachers in high school because I spent long periods away. Whenever there was a weekend contest it started Thursday for practice and extended until the next week because of friends and SD skate spots. I'd meet teammates from everywhere and shred all week long, driving around La Jolla to all the spots in the videos. The sponsored ams I skated with in CASL were leading the way in skating and the whole world was focused in their direction. They felt the energy and seemed to just spontaneously generate new tricks, like, 'oh that was easy, I wonder if I could do this too.' I went from tagging along with the Skate Rats to suddenly skating am with big names at contests and seeing the future in the raw, which was too much for me to handle- all because of George. Almost everyone on the line up for contests I skated became the most amazing pros of my era and beyond.

Being in a position to witness this all came about by accident (like it probably was with so many other skaters). It all happened when Little George took me with him to the Bronze Age factory in Inglewood. George had ridden for the company a while and was told by a fellow rider in Venice that Mike (the owner) wanted him to go get a package; so he asked me to skate there with him, and of course I said yes. To get there we mashed in the blazing sun through the sketchy part of Inglewood all the way to the industrial side of town where all the factories were. Before we went in to see Mike the office girl made us wait outside for a mega long time (standard for skate companies). Aaron Murray came out to smoke a cigarette and said what's up to us. I asked him in a smart ass tone if he still skated and he said, "hell yah man, I lost two fingers to that shit" (holding up his hand), "you think I'd stop now?" After that he seemed really cool. He knew George from before and talked to him for a minute. When we got in, Mike Cassel, the owner, asked George if I was good, and when he said yes I got hooked up with clothes (and eventually boards through Mark Partain). That's all it took. That day we both left with a hefty bag full of gear and I was suddenly sponsored out of nowhere. The shelves in the warehouse were stacked high with Bronze Age gear everywhere you looked. In another room were large t-shirt presses that had four or five revolving silk screens. All the printed clothing was done manually, so each one was custom. It was rad.

Mike was excited about us, especially George who he believed in so much (everyone did), and soon we were sent out with photographers to shoot ads and encouraged to skate contests anywhere we could enter and they would pay. George had already done the contest thing and seemed more interested in basketball than skating and traveling- already over it and only twelve or thirteen. I would try to convince him to go with me to contests I was entering but he never would. That didn't stop me from taking advantage of the situation. I found out about every contest and hit Mike up for cash to enter them. He was down. In San Diego I ended up staying by myself at the team manager's house and quickly made new friends. I hung out with some of the local ams and supportive older dudes like Tony Farmer (a local ripper from San Diego) that were super cool to me and showed a lot of respect even though I was a little shit.

Once my buddy Socrates, when he barely started filming, came to stay with me at Glenn's and enter the weekend contests. He'd always be down to drive mega far not caring because he half-expected his car to explode at any moment. I think everyone did. The thing was covered side to side and front to back with stickers and had been grinded many times. Cops wouldn't even attempt to pull him over for fear of the paperwork; if they did by accident it wouldn't be long before they took off during Soc's explanation about the condition of his car and fucked up paperwork.

We'd leave at night to avoid traffic and blast the Smiths the entire ride there, any other tape was vetoed; he had cassettes of *Louder Than Bombs*, *The Queen Is Dead* and the new Morrissey. Soc did his hair like Morrissey like thousands of other people at the time (so did his brother) and sang the songs while he was skating alongside and filming Kareem and Shiloh. Kareem would bag on Soc's filthy back seat and say he should throw out the trash that we all had to shuffle our feet through.

About every fifty miles we had to stop to put water in the leaking radiator so we had to have a few gallons in the trunk at all times, especially on long trips. It was crazy because we'd go even though I couldn't get ahold of Glenn (my sponsor who had the house), I just had his number memorized and planned on calling him collect on the way; so a few times when we arrived in SD we didn't have a place to stay before contests. Once when this happened and we had no choice a few of us slept in a tennis court, all huddled by the netting where we hung a blanket to make a tent. Soc's brother Mino and some other dude got the car, but the rest of us had to eat shit and spent all night on the concrete floor. Soc had the hugest, gnarliest bug crawl on him in the middle of the night. No big deal. We hardly got any sleep and woke the next morning stiff as hell and so cramped up we didn't know how we were gonna skate.

I had no idea where San Diego was until I started visiting there when I got on Renegade Skateboards, Mark Partain's company. He used to ride for Blockhead so when I was in San Diego we got to skate the team ramp complex that Omar Hassan was always ripping in mags. It was intimidating to skate but it was one of those ramps that stick with you forever because of the crazy ride (the hips, the spine, and huge drops into separate bowls). A dream ramp. As I progressed I imagined what tricks I could do there if it was still around. Partain ripped it.

Back then Mark had long, dirty, bleachy blonde hair and looked like someone from the outback with gnarled teeth and a brownish red face from lifelong exposure to the sun. I don't know why but I was always annoyed with him in one way or another. But when he put me on the team he ended up bringing me everywhere with him to skate regardless of how I felt. The first time we skated a mini together he told me before getting out of the jeep that I "better be good [at skating]". It was at night with shitty lights on the ramp and I tried super hard to live up to Mark's expectations and surprised myself by what I was doing. We sessioned it for a long time while taking turns between about five of us, but Mark was a snake so it took forever to get a run. When we were getting back in the Jeep he turned from the driver's side to the backseat and said "you ripped." That didn't earn me a ride all the way home though because he ended up dropping me off late at night a few miles from my house in a gnarly part of Inglewood.

When I stayed with Glenn (the TM) by myself I would wake up in the morning on the couch and watch him take the gnarliest bong loads, the kind where people hold it in and make funny nasal sounds trying to keep from coughing. Mark would take bong loads with him and do the same thing holding his hand over the mouth piece to keep the smoke in. A few times he took me with him to trade product for weed and I remember him handing over the sickest chrome blue Indys for a sack. I wanted the trucks so bad and couldn't see the logic back then in trading for what seemed so little. Because of things I'd seen growing up in Inglewood I associated drugs with death; I didn't know anyone who smoked and never had weed explained to me. Nobody knew shit where I grew up. Maybe if I'd have smoked early on I wouldn't have wasted my late teens working for what amounted to shit and a bunch of missed opportunities instead of skating and trying to go pro.

Glenn had a nice sized mini-ramp in his backyard and other riders would come by and skate while I was there. You had to drive to get to any street spots in SD so we mostly skated the ramp all day and plugged in flood lights that hung from a tree to session it when it was dark. One day a fellow team rider came over and I watched him do a frontside late shuv-it on the lower transition. The trick blew my mind and almost made what I was doing seem obsolete. I was trying Madonnas, backside ollies and five-0s to fakie while this guy thought way ahead and was applying street skating to the mini- so fresh!

Skating was changing at the time. San Diego was leading the way in progression all over the world back then and everything down to the way skaters dressed was a result of this scene. I wore shorts and high tops while this dude doing the late shuv-its had flooding, cut off khakis, low top shoes and a backwards hat. His wheels were way smaller than mine, his nose was way bigger and his trucks were hella loose.

I had to lie about my age to skate the contests (lacking the proper consent forms). This put me against the 16 and older guys who were already almost pro and all over the magazines and in videos. Needless to say I got creamed. I was fourteen and would be in the same category as Daewon, who wouldn't even touch the launch ramps in his run but instead would double flip directly over them. His lines were insane. He did the best tricks, like saran wraps to fakie and body varial fingerflip grabs over the hip. I was hopelessly outmatched against skaters like Pat Brennen, Kareem Campbell, Frank Hirata (who killed the contests doing frontside three sixty tail grabs over the entire fun box- mega far), Willy Santos, Mirko Magnum, Ronnie Bertino and Kanten Russel, just to name a few. I would watch these guys innovate all weekend long like it was a science fair- although I didn't know it this was the hotbed and pinnacle of skate progression for the entire world. But back then I didn't really know anything.

Ronnie Bertino especially made an impression on me, snapping fat nollies everywhere. He had long hair, braces, always wore hats that covered his eyes and rode blank, prototype Think boards with huge noses. Way before we skated contests together I had seen him in Venice front blunt an entire double-sided curb and pop out before it ended, right in front of the Hosoi guys (Little Man and Joey Tran) who could only say "Damnnnn Ronnie." It was one step beyond the previous generation that was all about ramp skating and style; I know I was sitting there like daaaannng! There's almost no way to properly describe the type of evolution skating was going through; it was becoming an entirely different thing based on street style. Sidewalk surfing had evolved to include skating stairs, gaps, picnic tables, manual pads, handrails and ledges.

Kareem Campbell was also blowing up and in almost every mag, getting lots of coverage all over the world. He was the king of contest skating and his personality was so big everyone knew when he was around- definitely one of a kind. Numero uno. He wore the newest World hats and shirts and his jeans would always be sagging almost past his double xl shirts with his belt dangling from the front. I could only describe his skating as glossy. He had so much control. Anytime he popped his board would swivel and curl, sucking up to his feet. He would leap over anything and point his nose down after his back truck cleared the obstacle. His flips would swivel in slow motion and his 360s were always stuck to his feet. It seems like there could never be another Kareem in skating, he was the original gangster skater. He'd be at all the contests I went to. The sickest one I ever saw him skate was all flatground in an outdoor roller rink. He was riding tall Blind wheels that seemed to be giving him more pop. Most people were only doing flat but Kareem put all of his friend's boards down, four or five sideways linked together, standing up and did ollies and 180s over them in between flip tricks during his run, and won it.

I had no idea that I was skating with most of the future pros who made up that highly innovative period, some of which are now running the industry. When you're fourteen years old it's rare to have any kind of foresight. Inside me as always was a feeling of inferiority because of my comfort level- I was always barely making it to the contests, sometimes with no idea where my next meal was coming from or how I was gonna get home to

Lawndale. I just went with it. Sometimes I'd get the train ticket paid for or a friend would drive, but mostly I had to wait a few days for a ride back. When I stayed with my team manager he'd bring me early and I'd skate the practice to get used to the course, but the guys that won it mostly showed up right before their heat- just ripping. As they skated I would watch with no food in my stomach and sweaty clothes sticking to my body, giving me the shivers. It was still sick though to be there on those hot days to compete and watch skating all weekend 'til the finals were over.

The most amazing skating went down at the end of the weekend, and it was always clear some skaters were in a higher class than the rest, like Willy Santos. Willy would just hover around the course like a genie. He would cab the corners of the fun box or big spin them and back lip down the ledge every time- he was just built to ride. He qualified every time for CASL finals and NSA. He was known for a while as the skater in the Gatorade commercial, once sporting a Gatorade everslick board to the contest. I remember he always had the sickest G&S shapes and all of his gear would be gleaming. Around this same time period Alfonso Rawls appeared in a science textbook doing a backside ollie on a ramp (demonstrating some aspect of gravity) and it seemed like skateboarding had no boundaries.

When I was in college I bought a G&S board from E.T. Surf because I remembered Willy from those contests and wanted to reconnect with that feeling. It was after I'd been off the board for a minute and I began again skating hard to make up for lost time. I felt like I had wasted a portion of my life in school while those guys never let skating become second and turned pro when they were supposed to. Slowly in college I started missing more and more school for skating, just like tenth grade and soon nothing could make me show up. I was gone. Recognizing my mistake, I went on the grind for the next few years. I skated the board like I do boards today, until it was chewed up, rubbery and nonfunctional. I was twenty and living in a basement converted into a tiny bachelor. It was in the back of a house on the Esplanade in Redondo Beach (practically on the beach). The landlord neglected to tell me about the rain before I moved in. My front door was at the bottom of two stairways and I woke up once to six inches of water filling my apartment because the drain pump in front of my door got clogged by leaves. The ocean was visible from two separate windows, one in the kitchen and one by the bed, so the spectacular view kind of made it less shitty, but I still dreaded any rainstorm.

After I quit school, I laid super low and skated as a form of therapy either by myself or with a friend who lived near Rat Beach. We'd always hit this loading dock type deal near his house that had smooth concrete. It was the foundation of a recently torn down house with everything cleared out and swept clean. There was a parking block down it that was fun to noseblunt and a couch next to that to do tricks over.

We both worked at the same restaurant and had a lot of free time. He had a little bit of mota and the *New World Order* video, plus a bunch of new skate mags for inspiration that we flipped through before we went shredding. I remember he could do huge pop shuvs over gaps and was always down to skate curb cuts- that was his thing. Late at night we could be seen on the Strand or in the Riviera backtailing slappy curbs and turning our trucks red from grinding the paint. They were good times.

I had a huge collection of cds from Tower and would trip out on music when I wasn't skating. The waves below would create an ambiance that would put me in a trance and I'd lay half asleep on a rock hard futon listening to tunes. I played music so much that several times I was told to turn it down by the guy upstairs who worked graveyard. The music resonated through the roof and penetrated what must've been a paper thin ceiling. He'd have the most irritated, condescending look, squinting as he asked me to turn the music down "again". What a dick. But that's how I am now.

Early in the morning the seals would bark in the distance and come up on shore so close. The echo made it sound like they were just outside my window. At night I'd sometimes sit in the grass out in back and stare at the black sea, looking at it like a magnet was pulling my eyes to it. I'd stare and wonder about the future, still thinking it wasn't too late to learn a McTwist.

Moving to Redondo wouldn't have happened if I didn't work at Tower Records. I met my girlfriend there and learned about the South Bay from all the employees. I got the job by some fluke and had to lie about my age and somehow come up with a driver's license for the paperwork. The general manager (who was so harry he looked like he escaped from a zoo) was so out of it that when I produced a CA ID card a few weeks later, he thought it was a license and was too busy talking to check the age or if it said driver's license. That's how everything ran there. The other managers were amazed when your cash register would come out even and believed in taking extra-long breaks, even calling in for extensions. They were true believers in rock and each one a living encyclopedia of pop music knowledge. The hardcore employees would even be offended by someone's lack of rock intelligence. They'd correct you if you were wrong about some piece of rock history, or speak to you in a condescending tone if you couldn't name the previous incarnations of a band or what famous solo artist came from it. "He *started* that band dude."

The rules were lax because everyone who worked there from the top down was a music fanatic or a videofile and did their own thing, expecting to be left alone (and they'd do the same for you). I was pretty out of it but even at 17 I saw those guys as characters, each one committed to their persona and stuck in a fantasy world that seemed out of reach and odd, but at Tower they found their niche. Records and videos were a huge business then. There was no internet and customers would pay anything for the latest cd or digitally restored laserdisc. I spent hours there looking at record covers or switching prices on CDs I wanted to buy, all while a 6 cd changer randomly selected songs playing in the store. I'd just zone out, with no pressure to work- it sometimes didn't even feel like a job- which was good because they didn't pay shit.

We had undercover security guards that tried to blend in with the customers looking out for people stealing. One undercover, Albert, was oddly out of place in Torrance and any thief who didn't spot him as security was stupid. There couldn't be a better caracature of a cholo even if it was drawn by the best Lowrider Magazine artist- here was the Original Gangster. He got along with all the employees and was sort of a street prophet that could quickly synthesize information and put anything into perspective. He was way smarter than he looked, always pointing things out about people they didn't even know about themselves. He would bring to light simple truths that the mostly white, affluent staff would become uncomfortable over. One female employee acted disgusted after he farted and asked why he just stood there in the funk, to which he replied: "you know you like to smell your own fart." It was so true. He wore a number of gold chains and had a big handle bar mustache and slicked back hair that he'd occasionally rake back with a palm comb. His pager was clipped to his belt and he was always checking it like people do a cell phone. One day out of nowhere a friend told me to grab a super expensive laserdisc box set off the shelf and pretend to return it to get myself a credit slip, and that Albert wouldn't care. When I did it I looked over at him and he reassured me, "just be smooth." Thanks buddy.

Everybody came into Tower and sometimes I'd see Daewon stroll through. He would roll up in a brand new Acura and walk around looking for music, tired from filming all night at World Park or jet lagged from coming off a tour. He'd always say what's up and ask me what I was doing and had I seen Soc and his brother Mino. A few times during that era I ran into him skating at World Park and saw him kill the place, even doing five forty handplant type things on the quarter pipe and landing everything involving flips over the hip. At the time he had just turned pro for World and I had seen his board at Roller Skates of America where Mino worked. He was beyond pro status when he got his board. It's almost like World had no choice- he was too good. To me it just seemed like Daewon had it made. At CASL contests his skills were otherworldly and I didn't question it any more than you questioned nature or the stars, it was just a fact of life. Daewon shined extra bright because of his association with Rodney, Steve Rocco and all the pros at World; the freestyle experience really helped the young guys with the flips. All the different influences didn't explain how freakishly good Dae was though. He was traveling all over the world using his talent to make money at 18 years old, while I was in a fish bowl of mixed culture and confused goals and perspectives, working. I couldn't help but compare myself to him.

My sponsor went out of business like a grip of companies did back then, all at once. Daewon was on the only company thriving at the time- World Industries (and it could've been because of him that they were doing so good). Everyone looked up to Daewon Song. He probably made quadruple what I earned at my job with just his skating, doing whatever he wanted; so sick. With Dae though it was like that, he was ahead of the whole world- way out in front- a phenomenon. That's why I consider myself super shallow at the time for not seeing what he was doing and getting inspired to skate. For some reason I couldn't see past working and hanging out with chicks.

Out of the entire staff at Tower I looked the plainest. I had no rock ambitions and was the only skater in the place. The only guys that I really got along with were the undercover security guards from the ghetto. I would trip them out when I flipped through the pages of a Big Brother mag we sold to show them Rick Howard, who was in the store at the time buying rap cassettes.

When I saw them smoothly nab people just as they were leaving it reminded me of that panicked feeling I had as a child after I was caught stealing, and the humiliation of being driven home by the cops. It was a relief seeing it from the other side and I tried not to look as they were escorted by.

My workday was insanely long and it seemed like my life was just passing me by- it was stupid. A subtle depression crept in without me even noticing. I was only seventeen. To top that off I had to take the bus to and from the place, which shaved a few more hours off my life every day.

The bus is like a rolling prison and that's where I especially thought hard about missing out on skating. I'd stare out the window and imagine skating along the sidewalk as the bus drove, doing tricks in my mind on all the obstacles, nonstop, no bales, like skating with your fingers on a table, or a cash register. The inside of the busses were hella grafitti'd up. There was writing on the windows, on the backs of the seats and everywhere you looked, plus etching on all the metal frames- way crazier than today. No space was neglected.

I started to understand how Shorty felt working all the time and not being able to skate with the same freedom we all had just a few years before. Money just lures us too easily into a trap. After a while not skating would get to me and my instinct would kick in and force me to head out for a session after work in the dark, without friends and clueless what the new tricks were. I just knew I needed to skate. I'd release a huge buildup and skate for hours having revelations about tricks and just tripping out on what I could do and how amazing skating was. I'd relate science to it, art, society, anything- it clicked in my mind that it was everything in one, or your ticket to everything.

It reached a point where work really began to interfere with skating. It was obvious too, my gear was always busted and collecting dust from lack of use and my shoes were way too un-fucked up. I still tried hard to push around though. If someone at Tower came with a board, I'd ask to ride it on my break and after work 'til they asked for it back. Everybody watching would laugh 'cuz I fell so much trying tricks; I really needed to skate.

During this time my good friend Socrates helped me out with a few boards and some Venture Trucks that I rode 'til they crumbled to pieces. He also gifted me some ridiculously over-sized Blind Jeans that everybody at work made fun of me for wearing. Within a few years of me knowing him, Soc had become inundated with skating and it became his whole life, plus he started getting paid for filming. He was a trip because he would sing Smiths songs while he was shooting Kareem or Shiloh and say the quirkiest things- he didn't give a fuck. Above all it was his car that distinguished him (like I said before). Along with the stickers around the entire thing, it had dents all over with busted lights, mismatched rims and different size tires.

He was raw, I'd show up to his house and he'd have his camera connected to the VCR reviewing footage while slumped on the couch mumbling in a totally made up language. Usually a few ams would be staying with him, sitting around with one sock on and a half set up board on their lap, watching footage and eating a bowl of cereal. They'd be about to break out to Frisco or some contest and I'd show up with no board and work clothes. I just didn't take skating serious enough or I was bummed that my sponsor didn't work out. I missed out on a ton of shit plus loads of night skating under the Galleria and at World Park (where Soc edited and transferred footy at night). The years just flew by too and suddenly I was 21 wanting to skate more than ever. It never stopped after that- school, girls, cars, everything became expendable for skating. The late bloomer; it clicked in my head to skate and down that road I went, following it anywhere, like an addiction.

Fast forward to the present. It's years later and I'm still taking the bus after owning a string of cars that all vanished somehow. At the stop on Pacific Coast Highway I sit and wait for the bus a few dimes short of the fair, thinking about what I'll say to the driver and if he'll let me slide. On the ground there's trash everywhere and the sidewalk is so dirty that it seems painted that way like the hardest rain couldn't wash it off. An ocean of cars passes in front of me and I can't stop staring at a tall, chrome horseshoe pole thing made for bikes next to the curb cut, wondering if I can ollie it. The bus finally showed up after taking forever and then just passed me and a few other people by. The guy next to me started cussing in Spanish and a lady next to him just shook her head and rolled her eyes, then started calling someone on a cell phone. Getting passed up is just one of the many things that can go wrong taking the bus. The other unknown factor is that crazy things could happen instantly and get way out of control, then everyone panics; and trust me when shit goes down everyone becomes gripped with paralysis.

Once when I was way younger some Crips got on my bus in front of the now abandoned Hawthorne Mall and basically took it over. It happened in an instant and when the first gangster got onboard he immediately started wrestling the small, Asian driver while two more jumped on and began to tag their set on the inside, harassing a few passengers and saying the name of their gang out loud, throwing up a series of hand signs spelling something. The driver struggled with the gangster for a while (who apparently wanted to drive away with all of us) and the shock of the scene momentarily caused a panic on the bus. The other two suddenly exited out the back, which made the one wrestling the driver let go and follow his friends by forcing open the front door. The driver quickly closed it behind him and began driving like nothing had happened, like he did this everyday. He didn't call the police or notify headquarters or even ask the riders if they were o.k. He just continued on like it was business as usual. In fact, I think he called out the next stop in a calm voice thanking the passengers as they exited and handing out transfers as he greeted the new riders. A black lady with no teeth sitting near the back laughed and almost seemed proud of the gangsters as she said to another passenger, "you seen them Crips take over this bus." Everyone was silent for a while as the driver continued on his route passing into Downtown Inglewood and my stop, Market Street by the swap meet.

These days on the bus, I fit in with all the riders. My beard is overgrown, my shoes are ripped to the socks from ollies, my board is rubbery and my bearings need oil. It's no wonder I write about the past when my clothes were shiny, new and plentiful, just trickling like honey out of the skate companies I worked for. Those days seem like another life. The bus is always waiting for you on a regular schedule through the ups and downs in life. It's useful for meditation because someone else is driving and you can just zone out as a passenger. I read The Celestine Prophecy on a bus ride to Long Beach years ago on the 232, the same bus I'm on today- well, most of it. Looking down and reading helped keep my mind off the ugly city flying by outside.

The only time the city was beautiful to me was when I was skating. The streets and buildings transformed when I was filming too and appeared through the lens like a Shangri la, devouring the frame. When I was 24 I became super interested in cameras and started tripping out on the skate clips I was getting; and I mean tripping, sometimes watching my own skating, stoned and rewinding the tape over and over 'til I couldn't watch it anymore (I'm not gonna lie, sometimes on mushrooms too just tripping on skating as seen through the lens).

And like a miracle or some cheesy movie story line it wasn't long after I started filming that I got paid for it, even though it was crumbs. My first job was filming for a little skate company connected to Osiris called Arcade. This is when I got to know SAD and Malcolm Watson really well- O.G. L.A. skaters. They skated all over the city. Sad is short for *Simple as Death* and just the fact that he was creative enough to call himself this is testament to his originality. I didn't realize it until we started talking about our childhood, but I grew up with the dude. A guy named Big Al, who kept a photo album of all the IWSR heads and local skaters from the neighborhood, recently showed me pictures of SAD and I skating a pool together. SAD hung out with IWSR as a kid as well and once driving through Ladera Heights with him I pointed out where Shorty used to live. He turned and looked at me while riding shotgun and said "you did hang out with IWSR." As if he didn't believe me before.

He's a sort of a ghetto philosopher and guru that defies any type of label. Once when I described the frustration I was experiencing feeling like I was going out of my fuckin' mind dealing with my baby's mom, he said "sometimes you gotta get up outta there!" He was surprised that I had hung out with Shorty as well, and I corrected him when he dropped his name and said 'you mean Maurice Payne'. We reminisced and talked about Bill Ward, another Inglewood legend who we both skated with. Bill had anger issues and always wanted to fight me, but knew so much about skating it was hard not to hang out with him. He always had me in a headlock it seemed and I remember being bitter for a long time after he tricked me out of My *Jason Lee Cat In The Hat* board, but we never stayed away from each other too long. When we were getting along we usually skated every day; he was the first guy I saw do fakie nose grinds and who had skate mag pages for wallpaper. I'm still looking for a letter Bill sent me from Frisco when I was sixteen after he had moved away. Somehow he got ahold of my sponsor at the time, Zorlac, in San Diego and persuaded them to give up my address. He was resourceful and real sentimental, threatening me in the letter saying "you better write me back faggot, or I'll kill you." My super good friend- I really miss him the most. His number was in the letter and when I finally called him we caught up and laughed our asses off about the past- it was sick. We had the best conversation and none of that teenage arguing and fighting we did meant shit. He told me about this girl he was living with and that she and him smoked way too much weed (S.F. has the crip); and also that he wasn't skating. Bill was always arguing with M. Payne too, but Shorty wasn't afraid of shit and he always punked him back and pushed his buttons way crazier than anyone.

Shorty and I saw each other a lot in Jr. high but never walked home together because we lived in opposite directions; but I'd see him all the time, usually hugging on a girl or something a few blocks away. I left the school from the south side gate near my physical science class, just across the street from the police station. It was a long walk and I would daydream about chicks, sporting a boner most of the way home from school. Nobody brought their boards 'cuz they might get stolen, as you had to check them in at the office where they always disappeared, but I did anyways- sometimes. Shorty never brought his board and seemed like he was hiding the fact that he was a skater when we were in school.

A lot of black kids at my Jr. High identified with Bloods from the area and it was the late 80s when Bloods and Crips were really going at it. Once after school, while walking home, a friend from my science class (who was a wannabe Blood) was approached just outside the gate by an older gangster. He was wearing a dark blue sweater over a triple xl white tee and had a beanie on (sticking way off the top of his head), with a jerry curl underneath that was dripping lines of oil down his cheeks and onto his sweater. This guy was fat as hell too, but somehow he blended in outside of my school. Another dude was in the driver's seat and he was in the passenger side of a junky ass Pinto, holding a forty-ounce in a paper bag. My friend saw the dude way too late to avoid him and was caught completely off guard when the Crip leaped from his car and said "where you from Blood?" He began grabbing at his waist signaling that he had a gun, which got my friend's attention immediately. My friend responded, "I don't bang." "You lyin'," he said, "you a little Blood." "No, I don't bang," my friend was saying." "Yes you do! Stop lyin'!" The gangster said getting angry and lifting his sweater to show his gun. My friend was frozen. The gangster had control and started telling him

"This is A-Tray Crip Gang homie, say A-tray Crip Gang's the hardest!" Seeing the gun, my friend had no choice but to say it. He kept telling him to repeat it, to say it louder! My friend mumbled it the first time, but said it louder as the gangster got angrier. The Crip kept urging him to repeat it louder and louder, and then my friend saw him start to pull his gun out and he booked it, darting mega fast across the street when suddenly he shot and there was a POP! POP! POP! One of the bullets ricocheted off the mailbox and the rest completely missed my friend who ran like crazy and disappeared onto Queen Street! Being not too far behind him, I froze when everything started happening and time slowed down. I think the car took off after him because I saw it parked down at the other end of the school when I crossed the street. It was insane. There was no mass panic from the gunshots either. Me and my friend who was being shot at seemed like the only ones cognizant of the situation. There were tons of kids everywhere but nobody noticed, as if time had stopped exclusively for us. It was like everyone was under some sort of hypnosis. Oddly, despite the urge to book it, I never ran or changed the direction I was going. I passed the liquor store on my way home in a trance while friends called to me from inside. I just walked home, went inside and never said anything to my family. That's how it was back then.

The next day I was excited to have some gangster shit to talk about and I was telling everyone the story (like an idiot), and when it got back to the guy it happened to he became upset and wanted to fight me. All I heard in class was "ohh, so he's mad at Gayton," from someone else and then I knew I was in trouble. His friends from his gang quickly heard the story and saw him as a bitch for obeying the Crip and repeating that 'A-Tray Crip gang was the hardest'. Word spread fast. I should've kept my mouth shut. Nothing ever came of it though, but being the only whiteboy on campus insured that plenty of other shit happened to me that was equally as absurd. Not to mention that my name is Gayton. What a life. I never really noticed how out of place I was 'til I got older and started telling my story.

Anyways, my friends and I would walk around the exact same area of Queen Street (where the shooting happened) on New Year's Day and pick up the empty shell casings from the midnight celebration shots. We would find piles of the same round from automatics as well as rifle and shotgun shells- sometimes picking up live ones- they were piled all over and we would stuff them in our pockets and show them off to friends. Queen Street was crazy. On those blocks in the 80's I'd always see breakdancers (Queen Street Breakers) with cardboard out and a boom boxes blasting in front of apartments, while they did head spins and crazy legs or pop locked. If you turned and looked down into the driveways while walking you could also see black girls doing double-dutch with jump ropes in the driveways of huge complexes, their braids and bright hair clips flying around as they sang a rhyme to the beat of their jumping.

I always felt a false sense of safety around that part of Inglewood though because crazy things happened out of the blue, and as a kid I had no sense of danger- I was still learning. It was like swimming in the ocean before I saw *Jaws* or before I read a Jacques Cousteu book on sharks and learned about the terrible, mindless things they were capable of. Downtown Inglewood was scary. Once for saying hello to a tall, light skinned guy I got socked a bunch and had my hat ripped off my head and shredded on the sidewalk in front of my house. The dude laughed as he walked off, like he had derived major satisfaction from doing that. Later another black kid knocked me out in a liquor store in front of my classmates after school in elementary, causing me slide across the floor backwards like some movie scene. When I sucker punched him in the stomach to buy time and run he quickly recovered and chased me home to beat me some more. Then later that day he and a gang of kids showed up at my house hiding behind cars trying to lure me out and jump me. It was insane.

Our place on Hillcrest, when I moved nearer to the airport, was way more mellow but still dangerous because of how close it was to Lennox.

Their gang had a vendetta for Inglewood gangsters. They were always out, mostly driving, looking for anyone who even remotely fit the description of a gangster. People like me wearing Dickies and a ball cap.

Random deaths happened all over the streets (and I still hear about them from time to time). It was totally real. People died and I never saw them again which created a rift in my mind; I didn't understand what happened so I tried to avoid it. A friend would just say, 'did you hear so and so died,' and they vanished.

One of the original Skate Rats, Mondo, was a constant reminder of how sketchy the area could be and that it was no joke. He had been shot in the back, supposedly by mistake during some random drive by, and his spine was damaged making him walk all crazy but not stopping him from roaming around the entire city on the daily. When he strolled by I'd say, "what's up" and he'd say "hey little man" not really acknowledging my presence 'cuz I was just a youngster. Everyone in the neighborhood had enormous respect for him. He had a lot of confidence and wasn't letting his tragic stroll get to him, but everyone knew it was crazy. After school when I skated the Stater Brothers parking lot on La Brea he'd usually come by and hang out with the Skate Rats. They had a cool little set up in the back parking lot. There was a jump ramp up against a four foot wall for launching over and a hella long, double sided, pvc slider bar. When Mondo showed up all the skaters (who usually lined the wall where the jump ramp was) threw up their hands like a goal was made, yelling MONDO! They all loved him and Chris told me he practically started the crew. As a kid I accepted his injury without really thinking about it too much, but now as an adult it hits me deeper. I realize now how truly fucked up it actually was to see a skater impaired by some idiotic, random shooting.

5

I got to stay with my Granny in Northern California a few summers in a row starting when I was about ten. It was a huge break from the city. I'd hike, camp, fish, swim– it was great. When I would come back to Inglewood I would have wads of dough because she'd give me cash to do odd jobs around her two big houses, like chopping wood or weed whacking or whatever. The first time my granny sent me home for school I went straight to the swap meet in Inglewood to get a ninja skateboard. It was thick, white and squared at the edges with pink wheels and a fat skid plate. When I rode by the police station on the way home the board almost slowed to a stop on a downhill because the bearings were so fuckin' cheap, and I just barely kept pace with my brother and a friend who were walking next to me. It just needed a little WD-40. When I was younger my brothers and I rode little banana boards around the block or down steep parking garages. I had always wanted a bigger board and now I had one. The whole complete ninja board was only thirty-five bucks and after I took the skid plate off and oiled the bearings it rode pretty smoothly.

I mostly got around on a bike before I started skating, sometimes riding insanely far distances and exploring the abandoned parts of the city where no kid should be by himself. My rims were always mismatched and the thing was always falling apart. A couple times I popped a wheelie and watched my front wheel unhinge and roll away in front of me just before the forks hit the ground and I ate shit. Skateboards were way less complicated. With bikes the tube would always pop or the seat moved and the handlebars were constantly misaligned. Either that or the gears inside the pedal assembly were tweaked or the chain would constantly pop. A few times as a paperboy I had to walk my whole route when my front tire exploded from the overweight newspaper bags. Most of my friends I worked with would've just thrown the papers into the sewer and went home at that point but I walked around Westchester near L.A.X. until after dark delivering.

At that age most of the skating I did was downhill through parking garages or hills, which was about all that my ninja board was good for. The Inglewood courthouse had a multi storied parking structure with a number of underground floors and the smoothest, polished concrete. It was abandoned on the weekend and my friends and I (on boards and bikes) would go up and down it 'til we were almost dehydrated. One time late at night a bunch of us were riding a few floors underground and a ghost just appeared in full, walking close to the wall! I saw it but didn't pay any attention, thinking it was a person (it makes my hair stand up thinking about it) until everyone freaked out, then I looked back and saw it was almost see through. It was an old man walking, staring straight ahead not seeing us. My friends were all so spooked they darted for the nearest exit, then we all joined in panic piling down the staircase and got out of there.

We got to a safe point and talked about it for hours afterward, plus everything else spooky that ever happened to us. This wasn't the only paranormal thing I saw happen near downtown. More than a few times my brother and I witnessed massive fireballs shooting down like comets in the night sky that came so close it seemed as if they were landing behind the fire station a half block away.

The most insane thing I ever saw as a kid in Inglewood was a U.F.O. flying over the top of the senior citizen home across the street. It was a huge dark grey, thin disc with black rectangles looking like windows on the side. The thing flew perfectly horizontal above the six or seven story building, rotating smoothly across the sky and took only three or four seconds to pass out of sight. It was low enough that bunches of people had to have seen it, especially in a crowded city like *Inglewatts*.

When it caught my eye I was playing with the faucet in my backyard and immediately stopped paying attention as icy cold water poured over my hands, and I became gripped with momentary paralysis. Then as fast as I could I ran in the house and told my mom! She didn't believe me because I had told so many lies up to that point (like when told her I saw pterodactyls in Yosemite with my dad), and just said "that's nice." Inglewood was a strange place back then.

I also had vivid dreams of hurricanes in our neighborhood lifting trees and suspending them horizontally in the sky while my mom and dad, unaffected, looked on casually like it was nothing; or other dreams of planes loudly screaming by at low altitudes during a crazy wind storm and being forced backwards into the ground, then exploding catastrophically nearby.

All these memories go back almost twenty-five years and just like now the bus was my only way of getting around back then. I can't believe I've been skating twenty-five years. When I was riding on the Torrance Transit from my daughter's house watching Interpol videos on my phone, I was texted by my friend Austin who watched a Ted Talk on You Tube given from Rodney Mullen. He told me to check it out 'cuz it had a bunch of footage I shot of Rod at the beginning. I saw it and before he came out to talk to the audience on a USC stage, his skating was playing on a movie screen. When he did come out he was rolling on his deck. It got me psyched and made me realize how much those long days of filming keep paying off, but no dough. It just gets respect in the skate world because somewhere I put in work to motivate the future generation- that's how I rationalize it. I don't see the time I spent filming Rodney as work, it was mutually beneficial. I keep receiving credit for the work, but have to try hard to convince new ams that I filmed what I did because they look at my gear and think I'm lying. They say "why doesn't Rodney give you boards?" I look like a bum to them- a bum that can do switch big spin flips.

When we went shooting, me and Rod would carpool and he'd drive to spots in LA that sometimes took an hour to get to, so he'd play documentary cds and guide me through 'em by interjecting and pausing the cd to talk which made driving interesting and the time pass unnoticed. He'd talk about legendary skaters he knew or complicated technical stuff concerning his new board shapes or truck designs. One time he was like [talking about the time he spent with Mark G.] "Gayton, the Gonz is funny but after a while it gets old". Also Rod would play the coolest U.F.O. documentary cds. *Those* were mind-blowing and made the hair on my arm stand up. One of the speakers, Chuck Missler opened up a whole new world to me as he went on about hyperspaces and actual accounts of the sightings and even abductions, the craziest part. He went into Roswell way beyond anyone I've ever heard speak on it. I would have to snap out of it when the car stopped because I was momentarily transported to a different reality. I forgot I had to film or didn't want to. When Rod would warm up we'd skate together, but kind of separately, and when it was time to shoot I still wanted to skate- work had to get done though.

The tricks I filmed of him keep getting replayed because of how technically advanced and different they are (but also he was on a hot one at the time)-

and of course because of his status and legendary history in skating. There also seems to be a bit of luck involved because Soc filmed him way more than me but mine keep getting played. Sometimes we'd shoot all day and come up empty handed because the trick he was trying hadn't been invented yet- but a couple were landed fast and we'd quit early, unable to continue after things came together so perfectly. Other tricks, like some that played in the Ted Talk, were re-filmed a few times to get the best possible make.

Sometimes, when he felt like he was getting close to landing a trick, he'd ask me to sing *"I Got The Power."* I would just stare at him, wondering if he was serious because it was the oddest request, but I felt bad and didn't want to ruin his mood, so I tried to say it, though I couldn't quite get it out. He'd put his hand to his ear like he could barely hear me and then get depressed and say, "come on Gayton!" It felt as silly as when I was a waiter at the Olive Garden where the managers would insist you repeat robotic monologues to the customers who'd stare at me like I was an idiot. I really wanted to motivate him because I wanted the clip as bad as he did, but it just wasn't me.

Rodney had such command of the board he only had to touch it with his foot and it would do all sorts of things. He'd nonchalantly talk about spots and new skaters to take your mind off of him while he was warming up with the most amazing freestyle tricks- plus staples like switch frontside heelflips and switch backside flips (then switch backside flip underflip), or the most popped nollie kickflip underflip. I'm not even going to try and name the freestyle tricks he did, but watching him skate in between shots was worth more than the measly fifteen dollars an hour the company was paying me and I only got paid when the camera was rolling. The same goes for Creager, Marc Johnson, Daewon, Marcus Mcbride, Lavar Mcbride, Gershon Mosley, Rodrigo Tx, Gailea Momolu, Louie Barletta, Chris Haslam, and especially JB Gillet. I got seriously zapped with the skate bug filming these guys and I eventually became more interested in pro skating than pro filming; but it was natural because I filmed like crazy for years and it seemed for a while I would only get psyched if I was creating in front of the lens. After about ten years though, there came a point when I just couldn't pick the camera up anymore- I was over it. I just wanted to skate.

  The skaters I filmed were inspiring me so getting tiny paychecks and skate gear as compensation for hours of work was more like an internship I volunteered for than a job (and I was always broke). On tour I would irritate the pros I filmed by skating demos and giving autographs to kids who thought I was pro when I skated. They didn't care who I was they just wanted an autograph. Creager got me started on it when he said to me before the first demo (on the Blind tour), "do you have your signature down?" He was recognizable worldwide and even kids in New York eating at the same restaurant as us approached him and said "you're Ronnie Creager" to which he replied slyly, "yah, who are you?" It was a blast hanging with him. I was having too much fun skating and was told more than once by pros to get my camera from the van and start filming.

Socrates gave me my first job at World. I knew him from living in Lawndale years earlier when we'd go to CASL contests together. When I finally reconnected with him it had been a few years, and I kept calling him to talk about movie ideas 'til he told me to stop by his place and talk about them. He ended up sending me home with two kittens and a promise to consider my movie idea.

When we were both way younger and before he started filming for World, he helped me out with a tape for my wheel sponsor (an Australian company named Cockroach Wheels [and as it turns out my house was infested with them]) who was pressuring me to film a video to stay on the team. I still have it. I was fourteen and Soc took me around on his own dime to shoot for a few days, and filmed and edited my vhs video that ended up keeping me on the team. Now it was years later and filming was blowing up. Soc had filmed hall of fame skate clips for years and a lot of the top pros owe him their careers for his dedication.

I told him I had a digital camera and that I could shoot and eventually he called me for a little work that led to more. On my first job he needed me to film Sluggo last minute for Daewon vs. Rodney Round 2 and asked if I could go to the Encinitas vert ramp to meet with him as he was too busy and going out of his mind editing the vid coming out any day. It ended up being a mission. I drove out with a friend not really sure what to expect and waited mega long for him to arrive. When Sluggo showed up he was with Colin Mckay who warmed up and within minutes started doing switch backside 360s perfectly along with enormous airs in his runs- a completely seasoned pro at the top of his game. The ramp was so tall it looked like it had over-vert from the top. Sluggo did a rodeo flip that I filmed from the deck hanging my camera down underneath him. He liked the angle when he saw it, saying that it was the best he could do it. He was super cool and had a smile on his face the entire time. On the way home we checked out Carslbad High to look at the gap and relive some Jeremy Wray Plan b lines. We filmed some corny stuff inside the school that I'm still looking for in my tapes.

When I got back with the footage Soc was pissed because I blew it out and he had to adjust the exposure. The World team manager at the time peeled me off a hundred-dollar bill from his pocket and they began adding it into the World Industries section. Soon after that Soc got me a desk job reviewing boxes and boxes of tapes of original World, Blind, A-Team, Plan b and Prime footage that the company wanted catalogued for future use. The tapes were mostly Soc's and contained the clips that had already appeared in World videos, but as I began reviewing them I found out that skate tricks weren't the only thing on the tapes. Like any filmer he had random stuff recorded, mostly personality stuff, where Soc would ask the skaters questions or just put the camera in their face and force an uncomfortable comment out of them; it was usually after they landed a sick clip. He'd leave the tape rolling for an insane amount of time after a make, so this allowed me to hear and see how the skaters really acted; I got into it.

On one tape Fabian Alomar grabbed the camera while Soc was driving and did a commentary from the passenger window- the world according to Fabian. It went on for about fifteen minutes as Soc drove around L.A. and had probably never been watched. Socrates is sort of the absent-minded professor of skate filming, and reviewing his tapes tuned me into a dimension of skateboarding hardly anybody will ever see. So many groundbreakers were just never transferred to a master reel and only survive in obscurity. The most amazing outtakes (or at least stuff I saw potential in) and first time landed on film tricks were lost on these Hi-8 tapes; Soc was too busy loading another tape to review all of them, and if the skater didn't bug him about it, he never logged it.

There were days where several legendary bangers were filmed within the space of an hour. Jeremy Wray and Lavar Mcbride, for instance, skated the Palos Verdes High rail together and after Lavar did about four tricks in close succession and his wrist was out of commission, Jeremy Wray took over and did a 270 lip. Dimitry was on the floor shooting photos and Soc kept putting the camera in his face, which irritated him. He filmed the whole thing start to finish. I got to see the reaction from the other skaters, the progression toward landing a trick and other stuff like the skater staring at the spot and sizing up the obstacle or trying other moves.

Logging these tapes became addicting because everyday I worked I witnessed classic tours, legendary sessions and the development of some of the worlds best pros. I felt like I had exclusive insight, as if I was admitted to a library of rare knowledge only meant for a few. Once when the daylight was fading on a skate session, Keenan Milton (when he rode for Blind) was still trying a trick when Soc told him it was too dark to film; Keenan got close to the camera and said, "Soc, I'll light it with my eyes." Another tape I remember seeing was of Creager skating an orange picnic table at an El Segundo school with Rodney, and them both taking turns filming. Creager was doing switch front blunts on the top and snapping huge switch frontside flips afterwards then veering off as an indication he was done- footage that was never released. Rodney was crooked grinding the whole table to a nollie varial heel out. This seemed like one of those perfect filming days when the spot wasn't a bust, there was perfect weather and the filmer was free to experiment with the camera. It must've been around the time *Trilogy* was being filmed.

Creager and Rodney had a good repoire and a lot of times when I filmed Rodney, Creager would show up and haunt his session, then leave unexpectedly like a hit and run. Once when me and Rod were filming, Creager met us under a freeway underpass to lend him some custom school benches. Somehow (as usually was the case) a group of skater kids found us and used a nearby red curb as bleachers, watching the whole time. Creager sessioned a manual pad while Rodney was close to making a front crooks on a table that he popped into a backside nosegrind on the bench next to it. As usual Creager was at it and just peeled off insane combos, like nollie front foot flip nose manuals and nollie flip nose manuals to nollie flip out, without any real effort, just miles ahead of skateboarding's state of the art. Half the stuff was experimental and you could see what he was getting at then he'd just leave it alone and move to another trick like a nollie crook on the red curb the kids were sitting on. When he landed anything they all threw their arms up in unison cheering; I almost thought they were doing the wave at one point.

Creager knows how to have fun skating and at the same innovate wherever possible. I felt like I already knew him before I started filming him because of all the footage on the tapes I was reviewing. I would trip out on the unreleased stuff in these archives. I was responsible for logging actual time codes and names of spots/tricks on a paper printout, never even sure that I was doing it right. Soc would just sign my checks and pretended to be psyched on my progress that he had absolutely no time to monitor. He would be so busy entertaining skaters and showing them their footage reels or editing, sometimes with Rodney or Daewon behind him, that he just never had time to look at my work. On top of this, Soc's wife would call non-stop and harass the guy about everything under the sun; a few times I saw him almost blow a circuit. The tapes were all there in boxes when I was finished but because of corporate schizophrenia, it was all logged over again by a different guy a few years later and although I got paid, my work was for nothing.

I saw Rodney around the office a lot (which was a wood framed complex lined with metal mesh for walls) and seemed to effortlessly get along with him, and real fast we started skating with him more. Soc usually filmed him but he was so busy shooting Daewon that he had me hook up with Rod for a while. Having the desk job reviewing tapes put us in constant contact because Rodney was always at World doing business. It was like an extension of the logging 'cuz he knew so much and I would always pick his brain when we were filming. In the field he'd be in a way better mood than around the office. Being in the streets skating was like real freedom to him- out there he was far away from any interruptions and felt the call of the wild.

I got super lucky with the angles on a few tricks we shot so I got more work filming and started doing way less office work. Rodney almost exclusively filmed on the weekend so I hooked up with a few skaters during the week that rode for other Dwindle companies like J.B. Gillet, Enrique Lorenzo and Marc Johnson. One thing I missed about the desk job when I started spending more time in the field was watching all the new vids that came in through the mail. I was inspired by R.B. Umali videos like E.S.T. (Eastern Standard Time) and a bunch of other skate vids that had so much soul in a time before skateboarding became too mainstream- just prior to the millenium. There were also VHS sponsor-me tapes coming in from just about every pro in skateboarding that I watched in between logging. Even if the pros were hooked up they still sent around tapes always looking for something better. World was cheap. They would get excited about up and coming ams that wanted to be part of the camp, but didn't want to pay them. I was there when they passed up Mark Appleyard, Rodrigo Tx and Chris Cole (just to name a few) because they weren't willing to shell out.

Just after the desk job expired all kinds of skaters who rode for World companies began hitting me up to film. I just fell into opportunity and my friends couldn't believe my quick progress into pro filming. The Pros could see that I had a true passion for skating and really appreciated my enthusiasm and ability to relate to their ideas and the confidence I had in their plans for tricks or lines they designed. Working in a building where the best skaters in the world flocked to didn't hurt. Whether coming off a tour or visiting from out of town, every skater and their momma would stop through Dwindle. Ex pros, new ams, salary pros, legends- everyone.

Just a few years earlier I started learning how to film in Long Beach with a nice Hi-8 camera that I took everywhere. For a while I filmed everything, not just skating. My friends were super interesting on and off the skateboard so I would shoot all kinds of footi. When I switched to digital I got help on angles from Dave Hoang, who taught me the *swoosh* with my one chip camera, which was simply passing the skater as he came towards me adding a motion and distance effect. He was filming Danny Montoya and Rob G at the time and was the filmer who most believed in Chad Tim Tim and compiled footage that eventually got him hooked up. He had master tapes of all his buddies' clips- he was super organized. There were tricks and lines Dave showed us that were never released anywhere and only his homies knew about, like a line Montoya did at Cal State Long Beach: Nollie half cab heal up three long steps, then a switch kickflip back tail one eighty out on the perfect concrete bench, where he just ate up the whole thing. It's amazing they even got to film there because it's such a bust, but those guys were on it back then, always taking advantage on holidays. Dave was cool enough to hook up the RCA cables to the TV a few times after skating and show us his whole reel, giving us a little insight into what kind of skating was going on in the cuts of Long Beach.

I started shooting more when I moved back to the South Bay and hooked up with Malcolm Watson and a few other guys for no pay at all. I was hooked on filming and I was able to borrow my girlfriend's car and scrape up bucks for gas money and just not eat. When I started filming Malcolm and Sad at USC I hung out exclusively in LA or by the beach in Santa Monica and stayed away from Long Beach 'cuz it was dragging me down at the time. Sad and Malcolm are so original that I didn't mind scrounging to get out to USC from Torrance every day. Going so deep into South Central spots we ran into some crazy L.A. shit, but that's nothing new- we survived. Sad would hold a white sweat rag in one hand while skating and filming and never let it go. He used to be pro for Gonz's company 60/40 so I figure the Gonz saw what I saw. The dude would always surprise me with his bag of tricks. Also, Sad always had some wisdom to impart in a confident, omniscient voice making every day interesting during the down times of skating.

Once at the Santa Monica sand gaps he busted a line in front of Mike Carrol and other Santa Monica heads that had all just come from relaxing on the sand, and sat to watch Sad film his tricks. He frontside crooked grinded the round ledges popping out in the middle, then tre-flipped on flat and finished it off with the fattest nollie back heel over the sand gap, confidently missing the second gap without even looking (I think he even ghosted over the corner switch). Carrol had on neon green and black shiny prototypes of his DC shoe and was with a tatted chick in a bikini that was impatient and wanted to leave. They all gave Sad props before taking off, psyched to see an O.G. L.A. skater get it done.

At the time Sad and Malcolm were filming for the upcoming *Gumbo* video from Arcade, which was connected to Osiris. Malcolm's skating really impressed me at the time and he was the manual king at the large USC blocks, where he was clocking sick lines in run up to his pro debut in *Gumbo*. My favorite line was a Switch heel manual, then quickly turning around to a nose manual nollie heel out at SC. His personality, above all, is what kept me filming him. And although the experience behind the camera eventually got me paid more, the money was a joke. I had to wait 'til way in the future to get just a few crumbs. It didn't matter to me though, I was doing what I wanted and finally free of school pressure.

Malcolm had opinions and insight about everything skate related and more. He was a veteran Visalia Skate Camp counselor- clocking almost ten years, probably more. I would send clips of Sad and Malcolm to Jason Rogers or drive to San Diego and transfer them at Osiris to be used in the Arcade video. I'd always bug Jason for skate stuff in exchange, because he hardly paid me shit for the clips. He'd pretend to care so I'd keep filming the guys and give 'em rides. When I asked for money or gear he'd change the subject by talking about how he couldn't control how many fights Tyrone Olson was getting in and that he was gonna kick Sad off for drinking; and how was he gonna get funding for the tour from Tony Mag. I didn't give a damn about any of that, I just wanted some kicks and a new set up.

My gear was always busted and I never knew where my next board was coming from. A lot of times I would be stressing about my chick's car too because it had all kinds of problems. I remember Malcolm, Steve Hernandez and Sad would just be chillin' listening to music in my car while we'd be stuck in traffic off the 101 unaware that I was shitting bricks because it was overheating or the gas was on E. I was so over it at the time that I didn't even say anything- just waiting for the car to die. I've had to cope with putting change in my gas tank, sometimes being offered money in line by someone who felt sorry for me, which I stubbornly refused.

I met a filmer named Ariel last summer in the same situation I was in when I started shooting, like I was looking into the past, except he didn't give a rat's ass about anything- hardly anything. No license, no insurance, three kids, no money, notha. I almost couldn't relate because the experience was so far behind me that I forgot about the struggle I'd been through leading up to filming pro for World. He caught my attention because he put the camera close up in the danger zone and always had to jerk back if the skater bailed to keep from getting hit. Ron Chatman would only let Ariel film him and they were always together at parks. He was dedicated to compiling and organizing Chatty's tricks and had several Rasta edits of him on his computer.

The dude was poor. The real world and the status quo did not interest Ariel at all. He slept on the roofs of bathrooms at certain skateparks- he didn't give a fuck. A few times after we had just stopped filming and both left the spot he called me saying he had run out of gas on the freeway and did I have AAA or could I come out with some money. I always felt bad because I was stuck at home and amazed I made it back myself on such little gas- almost vapors. When I had money or some herb I would pay him for his time (sometimes handing him fat nugs I grew). I was psyched about his confidence in my skating. All it took was a few bucks, a ride or a meal and he'd spend half the day filming me. I always knew he was around at a skatepark when I saw his lowered station wagon (when it wasn't impounded or out of gas at home).

He wasn't afraid to ask for shit and always caught me off guard with his requests. More than once he called me for a complete, or a specific size board or some pot- I felt bad 'cuz I could never help him, especially when I saw some clips of mine he shot. The filming was excellent and close up in the danger zone. A lot of times we ran into each other because he'd get so close. At first I had some doubts, and before he actually showed me the footage I wasn't sure that his camera worked at all or if he was schizo pretending to film, Lenny Kirk style. He thought that was hilarious.

My good friend Mocha somehow got a cell phone in prison the other day and called me out of the blue. He got locked up for 12 years and is about half-done. When I spoke with him he was excited about the rhymes he was somehow recording on two Playstations inside. It didn't surprise me. He was always up to something in life. I met him skating in Long Beach a forever ago, and back then (before the 411 Long Beach Metrospective) it was a huge bust and we had to be special ops soldiers to escape the cops sometimes. Anyone who skated Long Beach a lot in the late nineties probably saw Aaron at spots. He had the most balls of any skater I had ever met and his tricks stood out everywhere he went. The dude had absolutely no fear and could make himself try the craziest trick down the most gigantic gap or rail again and again, even if he got hurt bad- so long as the board wasn't broken he kept trying it. I spent a lot of time documenting this guy because I thought the work was amazing and what happened to him sucks so he gets a section in this book to bring his story to light.

Once I attempted to transfer footage of Mocha's from Dave Hoang (a well known Long Beach filmer). I had a one-chip camera that was slow to start recording from camera to camera, so I missed transferring some of the best tricks he had ever done. Somehow I left Dave's without checking. I was in the process of
making a 'sponsor me' reel for him. When it was done and duplicated it got some attention when we brought vhs copies to the Long Beach Trade Show in '98. It would've been much longer and gnarlier if I transferred the tricks properly. One was a

backside 50-50 on a beefy squared flat rail connected to a loading dock that dropped off eight feet or so. The rail was high to get on to begin with and when he landed the impact from the drop echoed a loud bang! Then you could hear Justin Reynolds and Rob G. in the background screaming "yahhhhhh!" The dude would ollie off a roof on request. Sometimes people would bring him to spots and suggest he do a certain trick, but most of the time he came up with something ultra-creative on his own, like switch noseblunt body varial. But because I wasn't pressing the record button in time while transferring I also missed the most insane ollie Mocha ever did, and maybe one of the top three craziest ollies ever.

Justin Reynolds brought him to this particular spot by the dock that he ollied, which was a rail on top of a handicapped ramp in the Seal Beach harbor; it didn't even have a landing. He had to ollie over a wall with a flat rail and way out to the right, over a patch of grass and a curb, dropping ten or so feet to reach the sidewalk below. It was insane. I don't even know how anyone could even see a way to ollie it. When he began trying it nobody thought it was possible, I could tell. If he bailed it he was tight rope walking the rail after he ollied, then jumping to the bottom. After a few tries though, as fucking scary as the trick seemed, we saw he was close and about to stick it and then out of nowhere he landed it- boom! Everyone went ballistic! He did it with only centimeters to spare, and we didn't stop screaming for a few minutes, caught up in the hysteria Mocha just created by pulling off the impossible. A few minutes later Justin asked him to redo it for a better angle and he suicidally agreed, but broke his board on an attempt before landing another one. Legendary.

Everyone who hung out with Mocha back then has stories about him trying the most insane tricks and sustaining major slams. One dude that held the camera talked about a slam on a rail that was so horrific they thought an ambulence should've been called! Then he'd just get up, grab his board and running back up the stairs say "that hurt." We filmed each other all the time back then. The subject on conversation was always skating and we really felt like it was important and that we had a future in it. I remember sitting on our boards at the adult school watching Marc Johnson's 7 steps to heaven on the LCD panel of my Hi-8 camera, all of us huddled around it trying to figure out the tricks. Back then there were no skate parks and every spot in Long Beach was a bust. Cops on bikes harassed our crew everywhere we went and when the aquarium was built (with a skate spot everywhere you looked) we spent all day dodging them just to skate a little here and there. If we weren't there or at Cherry (way before the skate park) we'd spend all day hanging out in downtown buying nickel sacks and talking about skating or looking for spots to film, on foot patrol, skating intermittently. We knew all the weed spots around there (way before clinics) but had to travel super far to get real chronic, which Mocha always had to buy because the black dealers around there thought I was an undercover- they were suspicious of any white person. A lot of times it was dry in downtown and we had to go to spots on the North side, that we'd only heard of, to get stress. Always on a mission.

One time I was alone at a liquor store and naively agreed to follow some gangsters to their car for weed. One of them saw I was buying blunts and said "you smoke chronic?" I said yah and he told me to follow him and his buddies and that he had some fire so I agreed which was mostly out of desperation because nobody ever had good weed- it was unheard of. He said he had a dub and when we got to his car just outside he opened his trunk, and from underneath the spare he pulled out a little nickel sack with hardly anything in it, just shake and a few seeds. I said, "that's not chronic," to which he replied, "homie, that's the *baby chronic*!" I told him I was just going to get a sack from up the street and hearing this he tried to get angry and said, "you gonna make me pull out my weed on the street?" I said sorry and repeated that I was just going to get it from someone else. Suddenly his friend yelled out "bang on 'em cuh!" They all just stood there. I smiled and started to walk away when the youngest out of all of them handed me his half empty grape soda and stared at me with a frozen smile. His friend told him to get his soda back so I handed it to him and walked away from the awkward situation. They seemed bitter but did nothing and just watched me leave probably thinking "dumb honkey". For years I told the story to everyone; it was a classic.

I always carried a Hi-8 camera around Long Beach when we were skating and sometimes we'd shoot non-skating or random things we'd see on foot patrol. About the only thing I could afford to do at the time was charge my batteries. When I first started filming I'd always forget to take the steady cam off, so when I put a fisheye lens on it created an earthquake effect where the vignetting would wobble. I hardly knew what I was doing.

On accident one day my friend saw something he shouldn't have while rewinding the tape. I was making a sponsor me video with Allison Castro and mistakenly left the room while one of the raw tapes was in the deck. So as soon as I walked away he began fast forwarding where he shouldn't have looking for more tricks to add to the reel and stumbled onto me butt-naked nailing my chick. I immediately pressed power and we both just laughed our asses off, but it was weird.

He was roommates with Fabrizio Santos (the Breeze), whom he called Caro de Sapo, which means 'head of the frog' because they thought he looked like one. It was Fabrizios first time in America and he was a shy little guy, practically pro already. He was quiet and I didn't really notice him until we were skating in Downtown Long Beach with a group including Marcus Bandy, and of course I had no tape to film with. He was frontside flipping off enormous roll-in ledges that were hardly wide enough to drop in on and landing mega far away. He nosegrinded the rail in front of the library first try and ruled the whole session without saying a word, maybe because he was insecure about his English. The Downtown LB Library has a labyrinth of these ledges that are tiered in some places and can be a grass gap depending on the architecture; like one at the very top that Mocha varial flipped for fun with no camera (the trick was so raw it seemed like he invented the varial flip right there). We'd loiter around these garden type levels and waste time and roll blunts of stress when we had nothing to do which was pretty much everyday. This down time was usually when Mocha's board was broken (which was all the time), because that was the only thing stopping him from charging it and filming the most amazing skate part, and I usually had charged batteries and tape to film on. He'd almost always have to walk home with his board in two pieces when we went shooting because he tried the craziest shit. The board would always break and he'd split the deck completely off the trucks on both sides so he had less to carry- it was routine. Mocha rode for an obscure shop called Area 51 and always got a hot setup from them with Web Trucks (a wild variation on the traditional skate truck). An ad for these trucks ran Transworld where he was doing a kickflip 50-50 on a dumpster from two huge stairs we frequented in downtown LB. He'd always go big. Another day when we were filming on the same blocks he angled a long wooden bench super steep down it and lipslid the thing with lightning speed (from high up) then 360 flipped off a curb less than a second later- every time. It reminded me of some of Marc Johnson's lines in *Seven Steps to Heaven*.

His brother Kyle would always be skating with us, sprinkling satire and irony on our mundane treks through downtown and beyond. The dude was funny. Kyle and I both got hired at the Long Beach Aquarium when it first opened. We loved weed so much we'd leave the place on our break to smoke by the ocean out of an aluminum can, which helped us deal with the Disneyland atmosphere of the Aquarium. It was stress with seeds but did the trick so we could manage the ridiculous work we had to do. One day I just never went back and asked Kyle to grab my check. He replied a little angry, "man, handle your business!" He kept it real.

I went from that job to a movie theatre on PCH near Seal Beach. I was an usher at first, cleaning up theatres and opening and closing the doors. I'd caught the beginning and end of *Saving Private*

Ryan, *Thin Red Line* and many other films so many freakin' times that I actually became curious about what happened in between. The first night working I found 60 bucks on the floor while cleaning up a theatre and thirty the next night; I thought it was gonna be the shit and that I was finsta be rich, but then I never found money again.

I made the mistake of doing acid before going to work one day thinking I was just gonna clean up theatres or something, when the manager decided to suddenly train me to work in the ticket box. Usually I just sold candy at the registers or cleaned the theatres and made out with the chicks there on trash runs. But the ticket box was sort of complicated and I was really confused and unsure if I could manage when it was being explained to me. Even though I kept fucking up and asking the same questions over and over, the female manager who was training me only got slightly irritated. She was about forty years old, had a gruff personality and squinting eyes inside a squared off face and almost no personality- so out of place in the world that I probably looked normal to her. I got paranoid and thought for a second that *she* was on acid because she acted like that normally, without drugs. I was peaking just when she left me on my own and that's when it started getting easy. When I got a little break I told my co-worker, who was in the booth with me, and she said, "that's what it is, I was *wondering* what was wrong with you!"

When I worked the candy counter I would give everything away because I thought the candy and popcorn and stuff were ridiculously overpriced and I was poor so I felt bad. I'd see family with kids and charge them for maybe one thing. I felt like

Robin Hood. But I always had a time limit on jobs and it wasn't too long before I got bored of picking up popcorn and selling tickets and quit the movies to skate; I couldn't stop thinking about riding and I felt like I was missing out when I wasn't on the board. Some people could easily handle both, but back then I had to do everything to the extreme, just like when I quit school. This annoyed my girlfriend 'cuz we were broke all the time. Skating had priority and I didn't have the discipline to part with even one of my days; I saw working as time robbery. There was too much to do and as long as I didn't work, everything was o.k. no matter how skinny I was getting; skating was the only important thing to me. I was broke, broke, broke.

Once, fishing off a jetti near where I lived in the LB, I came across an older cholo with a handle bar mustache selling live anchovies out of a bucket that was equipped with an oxygen pump. I was looking for some bait 'cuz my lure wasn't working. They were four for a dollar and I produced two dimes a nickel and a few pennies, asking him if I could please buy one. He paused for a moment annoyed that I was broke, looked to the left and right like the transaction was illegal and said, *"handle it!"* When I told a friend the story he yelled out "you didn't have a dollar!?" At the time I never felt like I was poor because I liked my skating so much and it gave me confidence, but as I get older I realize how difficult it made things for me. On top of this I became a target for police as they single out skaters before gangsters in Long Beach and harass you to no end, wondering why you're not working. So many times a scummy Long Beach cop took my entire complete or ticketed me for some rare offence no one but him knew existed, like *loitering for the purposes of grafitti.* Sometimes I felt better off staying at home; I thought at least there you can't get a citation.

My friends and I were always bored and we skated 'til we didn't like it anymore and could only talk about other people doing it. We loitered around all the spots in Downtown, the Convention Center (where skate trade shows are held), the Hilton by the freeway, Catalina Landing- nowhere skateable was untouched, not even the bank to walls behind the gargoyle hotel on Ocean. One day, Mocha, his brother, a few other friends and myself wandered inside an abandoned Masonic Temple in downtown. The only way inside was to climb up the front window and hang drop ten feet. It was in an abandoned part of downtown. We explored the basement first which was grafitti'd up from a rave held there, and also from people like us. The whole place was pitch black 'cuz there were hardly any windows and the power had long been out. Walking up the stairs we were already starting to get the creeps when a bunch of pigeons burst out an opening and spooked the fuck out of us! The place was filthy- all run down with debris everywhere like an area after a nuclear strike. We followed the main corridors leading to hundreds of rooms of immense dimensions, each bigger than the last. They were empty and still scary even when illuminated by a lighter, which was the only source of light we had. The place was haunted and just dorm room housing for ghosts.

Anything could've happened to us in there and nobody would've known. When we finally got to the very top the view made it all worth it. The height gave us a sense of confidence and control over our surroundings, something we never felt in the streets. After passing the joint around that warm feeling came over us and we began talking. We started in on skating and about Danny Montoya's *Rhythm* board selling out the first month it was released. Everybody was vibing on him at the time 'cuz the tricks he was doing were so tech and original. I remember anticipating his 411 part coming out, knowing every trick would be some type of innovation in nollie or switch; and with him switch looked switch. The few pinners we had burned fast so with nothing left to do we headed out the way we came in. I don't know how but one of my friends almost set the place on fire, and we barely put it out then booked it.

We always continued the mission 'til late at night until the majority of us would melt away, but it was still early. Further up the street we ran into a girl from Arizona (who was a ghost herself) asking for change. My friends were always open to strangers and never judged people they met and feeling this, the girl began to reveal a whole heap of stories, mostly about addiction, that took place in Arizona. The girl said she used live in a tent behind a gas station, addicted to crack with her X before coming to the LB and claimed everyone in Arizona was an extra-terrestrial. She set up some quarters we had given her on the sidewalk in the shape of an arc, just like the *Phoenix Lights*.

We all ended up migrating downtown near the transit mall where my friends, after saying please a thousand times, convinced the girl to lift her skirt (she had no panties on and it made her face twist into a shameful expression) and soon after she quickly disappeared into the glowing convention area off Pine street. Downtown was like a dreamland at night, or a dimensional porthole. Phantoms and apparitions would just appear out of the dark and vanish into the back of our minds. Sometimes we weren't sure if the person we saw was actually our friend or a ghost, because sometimes they were never seen again and nobody knew if they moved away, went to jail or what. For some reason at the time though everyone would be under a spell saying "yah, that's the homie" and go along with it, then we would question each other about who it was when they left and nobody knew a thing.

We were addicted to hanging out with each other. Anything that happened to us separately would be the topic when any missing crew member showed up- and they were all crazy Downtown scenarios. Each of us memorized the story or was there when it happened and informed the others that were absent of that weeks' news. Of course it became legendary as soon as it left our lips. I always had the camera around in case something crazy happened and tried to whip it out to catch it raw. But most of it was impossible to capture and something to just experience more than desperately record.

There's a park connected to the downtown library called Bum Park. The shelter comes out to feed the homeless, causing quite a few of them to congregate there. So many times we were unable to skate the ledges out front because the homeless would be asleep on them. The park was depressing and it was sad to always see homeless people. The square rail closer to the library entrance was famous, showing up in many skate parts. One of the first people to skate it was Guy Mariano who did the most raw switch nose grind and switch nose grind revert down it in *Mouse*. Once Mocha was walking home from working at the movies on Pine

St. late one night when he ran into Danny Montoya being filmed by Ty Evans for Transworld's *The Reason*. They had the whole thing lit up- a beacon for cops. Aaron strolled up, and being a good friend of Danny's was urged by him to try something on film- he didn't even have a board and had on his work shoes. Danny lent him his board and Mocha switch nosegrinded it five times, one of them ending up in the montage.

When I saw Dan Wolfe's biography vid, I was reminded so much of Mocha by what Dan said about Ricky Oyola (during a certain era) being his favorite skater to film. At the time I was sure Mocha could do any trick and his skills were up there with the best pros. I desperately tried to show the world, bringing his tape to Dwindle and providing copies he could shop around at the Long Beach Trade Show. He was filming with the 508 (the code in LB for a skate citation) guys and I would give him boards when I could, but somehow, in spite of constant encouragement by me and all the pros in Long Beach, he went down the wrong path and ended up in jail before he was 23. He was the glue that bound our little circle of friends from downtown together, and when he got locked up everyone kind of went their own way.

7

I was living in South Bay when all this happened to Mocha. Mentally, I was preoccupied and my life was a complete 180 from the times in Long Beach, save for skating. I was living in the suburbs and

Filming and skating took over my life. My car was my office and it had skate stuff everywhere inside. There were tools in the center console, mags everywhere, boards and wheels in the trunk and hardware rolling around the floors. I was 24 and felt like I had unlimited energy, but really I was just getting good sleep. Even though my ankles felt insane and my lower back was killing me from filming, I still persisted like a 21-year old. Even if nobody was down to go, I would always skate late into the night looking for any spot that was lit- sometimes just to set off my endorphins. While everyone was asleep I'd be sitting on my board in between tricks and could hear the city making noises like it was a living organism. Sewers were gurgling from thousands of people flushing toilets; electric lines buzzed overhead, here and there cars swooped by, planes rumbled in the distance and the street lamps were buzzing when everything else went silent.

Near the pier in Redondo was a spot that was in all the original Plan B videos called mini sans (mini San Francisco) and I skated the shit out of it before the city skate stopped the shit out of it. There was a downhill to it and the tile floor was good for popping and made it sound cool under your feet, but it was a mega bust. I was readjusting to skating and my head was in so many places. I felt like I was making up for time lost on the board, rushing and not really paying attention to my feet or respecting pain and got hurt really bad a few times just being stupid. I practically broke my ankle in a pair of oversize shoes when my foot slipped off the nose and rolled in front of the board off a ledge. I let it painfully heal on its own and for the first few days it throbbed and swelled making me pass out a few times. I had no insurance and nobody who would help me so I dealt with it. A few friends took me to a bar in San Pedro the second night which was a mistake because walking on it made it worse and I sat there with my eyes bulging out of my head trying to finish a beer in the worst sustaining pain of my life. It took two months to heal and almost made me go insane from boredom. On top of that I had nothing for the pain and nobody to get weed from. I was staying at my mom's and my sisters would make fun of me as I sat on the couch reading all day, or hobbled to the porch and watched our cat stalk squirrels. Here I was six years after I strayed from the board reading old skate mags 'til they fell apart, dreaming of tricks with absolutely no idea that three years later I'd be on a plane headed for the East Coast to film a skateboarding tour. If I knew that, the pain from the injury and frustration I felt from being immobile would've become insignificant.

I thought about how real Long Beach was compared to the South Bay. The dream was so much more alive there. It had way more traps and could get depressing, but in contrast a lot more skating going on, even if it was to get around. When I lived there Belmont ledges were really close by and downtown was about the same distance. At the time it seemed like everybody skated there- I remember Van Engelen wore Nikes and solo-skated the outside ledges that were in Richard Mulder's *Mouse* part. During the same time, I saw Anthony at Huntington skatepark do tricks like a frontside bluntslide across the entire flat bar, start to finish, and shuv-it out so naturally that his body hardly moved when he landed, like J.B Gillet. Skating was blooming and that area was an underground destination for up and coming skaters. Once outside Belmont ledges a friend of mine, who was a skate fanatic, suddenly said "Rodney Torres" and two people I didn't even notice suddenly stood out from the crowd as Rodney turned around and said 'what's up', stoked that someone recognized him. It was during Tradeshow and you'd see a lot of pros randomly around Long Beach; I saw Dune skating out of the grungiest part of Downtown towards the convention center during the trade show- I was smoking a joint in front of a friend's house and saw his spectacles from far away, almost not surprised that he appeared and said his name as he passed. My friends and I would always sneak in the Tradeshow and pillage; some of the booty included my first filming backpack- a blue 411 embroidered and padded pack that my friend nabbed but gifted to me as I was always filming.

The thing you had to look out for in Long Beach was the police as they had it in for skaters back then. The city was making big development changes and wanted the skaters out. Places like Cherry Park, near Ocean, (where there's now a skate park) were a complete bust. I always carried around a Hi-8 camera and filmed every day, adding clips to a master tape at night. When there was something to film I started shooting fast because I knew we had a limited amount of time before the cops or security showed up, so the sooner we left the better. When I switched to a digital camera I was back in the South Bay getting a little filming work from Dwindle and having to supplement funds with odd jobs in the meantime to afford rent. I worked at the Olive Garden and was fed a whole load of corporate propaganda before I was allowed to make next to nothing serving food and picking up sloppy plates. Way too many times they gathered us all together to sing a company birthday song to someone in the restaurant, where I would hang in the back humming and mumbling words under my breath. It was embarrassing. One big black dude kept calling me 'pimp juice' as he asked for refills of his strawberry lemonade. 'I like the service pimp juice;' drawing out and almost slurring his words. When he left he put a three quarters at the bottom of the ice in his cup for me to dig out.

I wrote the intro to a photo article in Transworld all about how miserable I was working in a restaurant. My buddy Seu Trinh needed text for a photo spread he was putting together so he hooked me up and let me write a small paragraph for the first page. I was allowed to vent about the absurdities I was putting up with to make money, like cleaning up sloppy, disgusting plates and dealing with alcoholics and idiots. I wrote about being suspended at work for something stupid and skating a bunch as a result. It gave me some hope that maybe what I was meant to do in skating was scribble. Writing always came easy to me. It's the poor man's art and you need almost no resources to do it. That's right up my graffiti'd, trash ridden alley because poverty somehow has become my religion.

Skaters among skaters at least have some common thread but in the real world it was tough for me to relate with people, especially because I didn't follow the major sports. I had to deal with the craziest mix of people and some of the folks I worked with at restaurants were hostile, competitive and unpredictable, always trying to confront people over petty issues and start fights. I ended up boxing with a dude over some bullshit one night and almost lost my job. The fight got bloody because he hit me while I had tongs in my hand and I blindly reacted by swinging them at his head! When he punched me it was like a fight bell rang, and some hidden rage came out- it was crazy. We wrestled to the ground and even after I told him to stop he kept coming at me and I had to punch him just to keep him back, 'til the manager broke it up. The timing sucked because the dude was just about to cash out a party of 15 people that, ironically, was a group of Redondo Beach undercover police. He collected the money holding a bloody rag to his ear, which freaked everybody out. Almost immediately he left the restaurant and after going to a doctor he went to the police station saying that I attacked him, but he couldn't prove anything and had to admit that he was lying as we were caught on film fighting (barely in frame).

Detectives came to look at the footi and determined I was innocent.

The video became so popular around the place that, after the police came to view it, everyone from the management to their friends and wives down to the ex-employees and customers watched it- everyone except me. They would close the office door and view it over and over, drinking beer and having a great old time. Ultimately I was ashamed of the fight and felt like an animal for a long time afterward. Secretly though, everyone who worked at the restaurant harbored a grudge against this guy and the fight instantly elevated my status among the crew. Bus Boys would come up to me and quietly give me props, saying I did the right thing and that they wanted to do it for so long. As I walked through the kitchen of the restaurant all the cooks across the line would look up and laugh, throwing their fists up and acting like they were punching themselves. Why is it always me? Anyways that was a long time ago.

The bus jerked and I woke out of my daydream. I saw three skaters on the other side of the street rolling along with backpacks. One of them formed a hardflip with one foot and it swiveled and flipped perfectly. They went the other direction and as the bus pulled away I stared at the restaurants along PCH that started zipping by the faster we went, all looking delicious. I'm in no hurry to get home because there's nothing to eat and I don't even know why I have the fridge on because there's no food inside- lately I've been slummin' it. By some miracle I haven't been kicked out of my place yet and I don't know what I'm going to do or where I would go if it happened. My whole family wants to take my board and smash it so that I'll accept responsibility and finally give it up for good.

When I worked at these restaurants I'd get the craziest message from the universe if the front door opened like, leave, be free. Jobs like that were what made me so psyched to go on skate trips and my motivation to organize them doubled after working a few shifts; and I wasn't above begging when I was only filming part-time. I remember begging Rodney Mullen for permission to go to SF one day after filming (later I learned to only ask on the days we were successful and got a clip because he just looked at me, almost in horror that I was asking for traveling money after such a shitty day) and I didn't care what it took to get out of town; I'd organize a trip and get pros to go that weren't even sure where I was taking them. Dwindle would give us hardly any money to go and got us rooms in the red light district in SF the first trip I went on. I planned it with Enrique Lorenzo, J.B. Gillet, and Corey Shepherd, and prepared for almost a week. They were the pros at Dwindle I got along with most, mainly because we all smoked. I was driving everyone up and we rushed to leave before the weekend, so it was a nightmare trying to coordinate everybody. The day of the trip Enrique who was a little older than the rookie, had to convince J.B. to go as he wanted to stay in L.A. a few more days and postpone the drive. Enrique is already naturally anxious so this caused him to get those crazy eyes and become almost unresponsive for an hour until J.B. relented. After getting clothes and boards from the back, we first went to the other Dwindle warehouse up the street (where the board and wheel printing happened) to pick up J.B.'s new pro model. The shape had a steep nose and tapered tail with a graphic of the Soccer World Cup on it.

They were hot off the press and the warehouse manager was putting the graphics on when we arrived. He shook J.B.'s hand and introduced himself as he handed him ten decks in a Dwindle board box.

Everyone called him the "rookie." He was just 21 with one of the cleanest, innovative, gangster styles in the industry. Everyone was fascinated with him at the time- his technique and trick selection was a brand new, focused style that was one in a million and the most original to date. I'm still influenced by it and catch myself thinking back to that time always. I knew that I was around someone who represented the advancement of humanity and was untouchable and at the forefront of the skate industry, with skill that never ceases to amaze me when I think of it.

Before we headed out for SF I had to pick up Corey Shepherd from Orange County where he was staying with Rune Glifberg and a few other people. They smoked tobacco with weed out of the bongs in the house so anyone that didn't mix herb like that got a numb feeling on their lips and bad nausea after hitting it. While I was there some guy came by to trade Corey weed for skate stuff and brought his girlfriend and a buddy by to see a real sponsored skater. He said, "see babe this is Corey, he rides for Blind," and the girl nodded in approval as Corey said hello and handed the guy a board for a shady dub, then they shook. I had a tobacco ring on my face from Corey's bong and ruined my shirt trying to wipe it off. After playing his PS2 for another half-hour, we put Corey's gear in the car and headed to LA to pick up Enrique and J.B.

Corey clicked with Enrique immediately because they'd both been playing the same video game and Corey was eager to get back to it. I spent another half hour or so watching them both play while we passed spliffs. Enrique, being from Spain, preferred the tobacco spliff and I even got to like it on the trip because all three of them would only have it that way- foreigners.

It was another hour or so before we got on the road and we still had to pick up J.B. in Santa Monica before heading to S.F. When we got to his place J.B. commented on my haircut and said in his French accent, "got a haircut for z'trip," smiling and making me realize that the trip was the reason I had done it. We both laughed at almost anything each other said- he was living in his prime as a skateboarder and he invited anyone to enjoy that confident energy. His French upbringing gave him a sarcastic bent that saw everything happening in life as ironic and laughable. He was always smiling and pointing out the comedy in anything that happened, and constantly commented in a French accent, "man zis is crazy." We stuffed the trunk with an unbelievable amount of gear that caused it to pop like a jack-in-the-box when it was unlocked. The freeway was clear because it was so late and we listened to Ghotface's *Supreme Clientelle* the entire way. It just came out that week and J.B. couldn't get enough of it. The album ended up being one of my favorites for a long time after, and I still listen to it reminiscing about the past. When we drove over the grapevine and headed into the stretch of funky cow farms, J.B. told us about driving on the 101 at the same time of night with Jason Dill years earlier when a U.F.O. flew over them. It was written up in Big Brother at the time and hearing the story made us all look up for moving lights. I kept trying to imagine what it looked like because the description was no substitute for the real thing; seeing it for yourself changes everything, so I kept my eyes peeled.

We got to the motel at five a.m. and had trouble checking in because the name on the credit card was the C.F.O.'s at Dwindle and the team manager didn't tell us this. After naming all the people I could and almost giving up, he recognized the last name I gave and let us have the keys to an upstairs room. There were gay prostitutes with exaggerated handle bar mustaches standing in front of the room next door smoking cigarettes, completely indifferent to our arrival. We got a cot and I volunteered to sleep on the floor- we were all hella exhausted from the long trip and crashed. All I could smell was smoke from the spliffs because I pulled my hoodie over and it was reeking from the stuff; but after all that craziness I didn't care about shit except sleeping and the floor felt like a luxury bed. I was done.

At about ten a.m. I got up because I couldn't sleep on the floor anymore and was getting a cramp in my neck. Everyone else was asleep so I took off and walked around looking for a coffee shop. Coming down the stairs I glanced over to make sure the car was still there. The area was like New York with tall buildings, trollies in congested traffic and people walking everywhere. I got back with my coffee and started up the stairs when I heard someone yelling, "Corey!" over and over. At first the yelling blended in with the city noise, but after a while it registered in my consciousness and I realized the odds were too high and that he could only be yelling for Corey Shepherd. I said "Corey

Shepherd?" and he said super excited, "Yah! Do you know Corey?" I told him to come up so he rushed over and started explaining who he was. The dude was super psyched he found the place because he skated and bussed it all the way from Haight Street and didn't know where he was gonna look when he got there- the dude just had good luck. Corey wasn't even awake and Paul and I talked about Canada and SF skaters 'til he got up. When he saw Paul he immediately said "Zoltan!" Watching them interact was a trip. Paul was childishly compliant with anything Corey said or did and he could tolerate all the pranks and verbal abuse he was capable of. He hung out and played video games with us for about an hour before dragging Corey off to Haight where he was staying with his girlfriend and Karl Watson.

Corey had given Paul a vague description of where we were going to stay before he left and somehow he found it. He called him Zoltan because it was Paul's real last name, and he'd drag out the pronounciation like a smart ass saying Zooollll*tan*. He was dwarfed by Paul, who was 6 and a half feet tall, making me think of a parable I read about where an intelligent dwarf is on the shoulders of a blind giant who accepts all the commands of the dwarf because he had no other choice, (which is like the intellect trying to control the gigantic will). This was their California adventure. Corey had just recently got hooked up on Blind and moved to Orange County to show Americans how Canadians could shred. It was no joke either because Corey could throw down like nobodies business with an almost endless list of surprises in his trick bag.

Going to stay in Haight worked out better as Corey was the new recruit and didn't really know J.B. or Enrique. The three of us had been hanging out for a while in LA. and could tolerate each other- barely. We said we'd meet up with him at Pier 7 later in the day after we ate some food and went by F.T.C. When they left we smoked a bunch of spliffs and watched T.V. for a while before taking off, then piled into the car and searched for somewhere to eat. After lunch we stopped at Macy's where J.B. bought some new Polo Jeans he'd been looking for that totally fit his *gangster* style. I glanced at some of the prices and got depressed and thought about how I wasn't getting paid shit to film, then just shook my head and blocked it out. When we got to Pier 7 J.B. was given a royal welcoming by every pro in S.F. They all remembered him from a few years back when he lived there- this time he was received like a star.

Within minutes of being there, in pure synchronicity, I heard a loud voice echoing from far away and thought it was nothing until J.B. yelled out "Sancho" and Henry Sanchez came walking up excited to see J.B. He recognized him from far away and said "Frenchy!" over and over, hugging him and asking "where the fuck" he'd been. They sat on the blocks catching up with each other for twenty or thirty minutes. J.B called him Sancho and it helped me match the face because Henry just walked up wearing headphones like any ordinary person. (I didn't realize how much respect J.B. had for him and failed to immediately make the connection between their styles. It was only later when Creager wouldn't stop mentioning Henry and playing videos of his skating that I really understood how much influence he had on all the pros from his generation. Ronnie loved his skating, and I could tell Henry meant a lot to him).

To me he just looked like some ordinary street dude rolling up to Pier 7 until J.B. lavished so much attention on him and kept repeating his name, then it hit me like 'what an idiot, this is Henry Sanchez!'; I could tell Henry had mega love for J.B. and really missed him, I mean really- they were super bros. All the pros (like Rob Welsh and Marcus McBride) had the same enthusiasm for him and were excited that he was back in S.F., like the man was back. They were throwing down a virtual red carpet and all paying tribute. I just think of how much insane ripping they'd seen to have such a faraway look in their eyes when they talked to him, like they saw him walk on water. He made the whole place buzz, like a bee-hive had been shaken up.

A little while later Lavar showed up to the Pier with no board and asked if he could have mine (which was his pro model); I said no because I only had one pair of trucks, but I wish I could've in retrospect- it belonged to him, it was his pro model. Shooting with him would have to wait 'til we met up in L.A. a year or so later because he just disappeared after that. It was sunny and not so windy yet, perfect weather. I filmed Marcus do a switch ollie over the manny pad to drop and immediately switch crook the next ledge, skating so fast it was hard to keep up. We got a couple and I asked him if he liked it while we watched the footage on my camera's fold out screen, and he said "not really." He was trying to get a switch back tail after the crooks and knew he could do better, or maybe my angle sucked and that's what he meant by 'not really'. A few minutes later Enrique threw his board into the bay after missing a switch back tail up the blocks too many times. It ended up being a bitch getting him more trucks. I guess it was a bad day for switch back tails. Nick Lockman walked up and saw J.B. and they both talked for a while. J.B. had just turned pro and anyone that knew him was excited; he left Frisco an am and this was his first time back since then. It seemed like every skater from S.F. came through to Pier 7 that day to say what's up: Karl Watson, Shelby, Shamil Randle, I think Mike York. Nick Lockman got us some fire weed and we ended up rolling spliffs all day, sitting on our boards in the corner of the spot passing around a double paper baseball bat. This was before Pier became a huge bust and was torn down and it was a virtual party every day. Skaters from all over the world gravitated there. Corey came by with Paul to film and was over it really quick after slamming too many times on a bluntslide to fakie up the Pier block he was trying in a line. The few he did land looked sick though, and I wish he had done the line. It would take a few months, but eventually as we kept filming he broke out his whole bag of tricks. Crazy stuff hardly anyone did like switch backside noseblunts, switch backside 180 nosegrind reverts, consistent switch kickflip back tails, switch three sixty flips, and switch varial heels down anything- and the list went on. I suspected after a while that he didn't even know how many tricks he could do.

That night we went to an artsy hip hop party with free booze in an upstairs/downstairs loft, all packed in like sardines. Everywhere I looked there were art pieces on the wall and sculpture things on tables and in nooks and crannies. We stood in a row up against a wall next to Rob Welsh and Henry Sanchez, just nodding our heads to the music and watching the steady river of people walking back and forth in front of us. Henry Sanchez was drunk and mumbling a non-stop freestyle that continued the whole night; even if you tried to say something to him he would just smile and keep rapping looking straight at you. Rob Welsh was feeling good and proudly said to me "when my Aesthetics part drops…" then just shook his head yes like watch out. When I First met him he thought I was Dan Wolfe and asked if anyone had ever told me that. Rob had a super-confident energy and was a big part of the scene in SF. That week I saw him doing cabellerials to switch nose manual on the Pier 7 blocks, finishing up his new part. J.B. spotted him doing it first and said in his Frenchy voice "damn, that's crazy." Later in the week he bought me lunch when he saw that I wasn't eating- just a super-cool guy. Rob said he hated when people didn't have money to eat and gave me five bucks to get a burger. He pointed to the burger stand and gestured for me to go 'cuz he saw I was a little hesitant. The trip was on a shoestring budget and I was watching what I spent, conserving money for gas home and that really helped save the tour.

After the party we walked to the car downhill and Corey was so drunk from the free beer he kept calling Enrique an asshole and asked me why he was such an asshole and I just laughed because I thought it myself as Enrique could be way difficult. He's from Barcelona, the snooty part of Spain. I never held it against him. We all have some shit wrong with us. On the way back to the motel, J.B. wanted Philly cheese steak and knew of an all-night spot in the Tenderloin. Enrique kept saying no but J.B. insisted, saying loudly "PHILLY CHEESE STEAK! "

The next day we met up with Rob at F.T.C. looking for Corey's box which Dwindle was sending to the shop. Before we left motel room I remember seeing J.B. get up early in the morning and test a new deck on the carpet; as I looked up at him from my spot on the floor he said in his French accent, *"new board everyday"* and laughed. When we got to FTC the new shop video was playing, and while J.B. and Enrique looked around Matt Hensley walked in anonymously looking at the decks decorating the walls- nobody even knew it was him. I introduced myself and pointed out his H-Street board on the wall of fame. When he saw it his eyes lit up and an old grin came across his face. I told him about years earlier when me and him went with a couple of chicks to a Reverend Horton Heat show at the Roxy in Hollywood. It wasn't 'til the end of the night that I realized he was Matt Hensley because he was dressed completely different than his *Shackle Me Not* and *Hocus Pocus* parts. In between the opening act and

Reverend Horton Heat we got to talking about skating when the girls were off getting drinks and like a shape-shifter that David Icke describes, he morphed into "Matt, Who? Matt, Matt Hensely." I was blown away when I realized who he was and the girls made fun of me for getting so excited, but they had no idea how much I irritated my family watching *Shackle Me Not* over and over as a kid. Matt was with a girl named Tracy at the show, who he met through Big Brother Magazine where she worked, and was staying at her house in Venice. We ended up there after the show and she had *Barbarian's at the Gates* in the VCR, which Matt had never seen; he was freaking out about the *European Vacation* song in the intro because he had been looking for that tune forever in record shops and couldn't find it.

Matt was in S.F. with his band Flogging Molly and tripped out about the story I told him. When he left, Lavar walked in with Lennie Kirk. Lennie had a crazy look on his face and went to the counter with a bunch of Speed Demon berring packs trying to get money. Lavar stood watching the video screen zoned out not saying a word, wearing one white tennis glove, which made everyone compare him to Michael Jackson after he took off. He was a child skate star all grown up now and half-abandoned by the companies that sponsored him when he was younger. After a bunch of misunderstandings there was a big communication breakdown and he was finally kicked off Dwindle for missing a plane flight to an East Coast tour, after holding Blind down for years with just him and Ronnie. It was sad because everyone loved how he skated and the tour stories about him were legendary and almost unbelievable. Even guys from over seas would give him credit. They considered him an American super star, baffled that this could happen to such an influential skater, but like Jason Jesse says in *V-Day*, "they're all disposable heroes". Lavar's part in *Trilogy* was mostly lines and he was as consistent as it seemed on film- way more powerful of a skater now that he'd become a man and got booted in his prime. He was just like a lot of the pros I met through filming at Dwindle: insanely good and on another level, almost rendering all other skaters obsolete.

He loved weed and once while we were driving to a spot I saw him break some up and roll a joint in one hand, looking away while he did it asking me "you smoke?" To which I replied "hell yah!" Several pros told me that on U.S. tours he would buy up weed at demos making it so that nobody else could get any, and was hella stingy about sharing. On one tour he showed Seu Trinh (the photographer on the trip) a huge bag of mushrooms he was doing and, according to Seu, would wait in the van 'til all the other pros were done skating, then go out and do every trick they had done, switch stance. No film crew reenactment could equal what went down on those tours and nobody could measure how much it expanded the consciousness of skating. Skateboarding wasn't prepared for the adult Lavar. It wanted Lavar as a teen, in love with Wu-Tang and fighting off rival kung-fu opponents eager to steal his title.

Lavar left FTC with Lennie and we took off to give Corey his box on Haight Street. Gabe Morford pulled up out front and I asked Rob to introduce me and somehow I got his number to hook up the next day. I called the next morning after we ate at some expensive pancake house on

Haight Street. I hit up Gabe from a payphone but had to call back as he was hung over from the night before and wasn't answering. We hooked up really late in the day at the Alameda skatepark, which was next to an abandoned naval base. While Gabe skated the tranny we checked out the ledges inside and I somehow poached a line J.B. did first try (he later made fun of me when he saw it saying, "save the tour!") The blue gap to rail Cairo Foster lipslid in a Transworld video was near the ledges and we checked it out. The gap was insane! That anybody even had the balls to attempt it blew my mind because there was some serious hang time between the gap and the rail. I didn't see the footage 'til way later and the angle hardly expressed the true distance he had to gap out, or how hard the trick actually was.

After Gabe was done skating the park we buzzed around to a few spots that nobody was interested in. Frank Gerwer, who was with Gabe and Nate Jones, tried to kickflip a loading dock over dirt, but got fucked up in the process so he just quit trying. Frank thanked me for filming, nursing his bloody hands as he offered me the clean part to shake. Corey did the sickest pop shuv-it into the dirt but wasn't into skating the entire thing. We went to a few other spots and were about to call it quits until J.B. mentioned the plaza under construction across from Pier 7; he had just remembered he wanted to skate it and we signaled Gabe to pull over, (because this was still the pager era and nobody had a cell phone). He followed us and we met at the ledges, which had no landing so a wooden plank had to be put down over an open pit forcing the skaters to thread the needle when rolling away. Corey began trying a backside tail out over the double set and

J.B. followed him with a switch five-o 180, landing it almost immediately after a prolonged grinding sound, his Ventures just eating up the block. The ledge was meaty and J.B. charged it with no hesitation, locking in with precision and remaining almost perfectly still before he popped out like Batman. Gabe got his camera and Nate and Frank held flashes and set up strobe stands, heckling the skaters the whole time. After J.B. did the switch five-o he switch tailed the ledge three or four times going mach speed before he landed in line with the plank. I had to change the tape in the middle of filming and I handed it to Zoltan, who was there with the assist, and quickly put a new one in to continue shooting. Corey lost interest in trying the back tail even though he had slid the entire way more than a few times so J.B. quickly did it to fakie making Corey bitter and causing him to walk off- J.B. commented in his French accent, "someone had to do it." Enrique did a switch crooks that ended up in Slap Magazine a few months afterward, and J.B.'s footage ended up first in the *Deca* video, then recently on a YouTube compilation of his footage that I really liked and possibly in the Lordz and Cliché fliks. The clips made the trip and we only filmed a few things after that. He kept joking with me saying, "save the tour!" because I was complaining that we needed more shots to bring back to Dwindle so they would send us on other trips and sign my paycheck. Those guys were already payed and couldn't understand how broke I was.

The next day J.B. did a line at Pier 7 he shot with a filmer named Victor for the upcoming FTC video. Enrique told J.B. he should film it with me, but he said Victor would give it straight to the shop and he wanted something to be in the video before the deadline. As they were shooting there was a misunderstanding about when J.B. was coming and the filmer missed the roll up to the first trick, barely catching it as he snapped a fakie nosegrind popped out huge to revert where both sets of wheels hit the ground at the same time upon landing. He cruised around and did a fat nollie backside 180, then a switch 180 nose manual 180 out (J.B.'s signature trick) up the big side of the blocks. I just stood to the side while J.B. filmed and talked with Shamil Randle who was drinking a beer on the secluded end near the entrance to the pier. Dudes would chill there in huge indented, concrete windowsills that they also stashed their stuff in while they skated. There was a lot of good energy at Pier 7 and the people and vibe got me super psyched to be there, especially during that era in the history of skating. I thought 'this must be the place.' The brand new Axions I had on gave me a huge blister that made it hard to push around but I just powered through it and skated anyways with band aids on my heals covered by duct tape, which rubbed off after about thirty minutes.

The next day we had to check out by noon so we packed our gear into the car and headed out, stopping to meet Nick Lockman at his place near the Pier to trade all our boards and stuff for some more weed to cushion the trip home. On the way out J.B. remembered he wanted to switch tail to switch heal the ledge over double set, but Enrique protested that we were already on the road and claimed he wouldn't do it anyways if we stopped- such a pessimist. J.B. interjected, "save the tour!" and we drove out over the Golden Gate towards L.A.

When I got back to Dwindle, Daewon and everyone was psyched on how much footage we clocked and I remember Jesse Martinez in the editing room watching the footage with us and chastising the skaters for not producing at some of the spots. It was all shot with a one-chip Sony and soon I was promoted to three-chip status and sent on tours further out and longer with more per diem. It felt like things were going right. I had money in my pocket for the first time in a while; new equipment, clothes. Dwindle paid me to film their riders unlimited. 411 video magazine hooked it up by giving me openers (tricks that appeared in slo-mo at the start of the vid) which paid $200 each, and also for other clips of mine they accepted for montages and stuff. For a while Dwindle offered pay for publicity promo stuff like that so it started to work out that I got double paid for some footage plus bonuses.

8

It's hard to think about old tours when my gear is so jacked up right now. I was living in a time of real decadence and hardly aware of it. When I've ollied my shoes to death and I'm unshaven, people mistake me for a bum as I step off the bus. I own one pair of pants, one shirt and one sweater- a rich man in some countries, but in L.A. people are so deluded by vanity that I get stared at like, 'that poor homeless man?' My board, bearings and shoes are screwed but it doesn't bug me, if it did that would show my lack of faith. It's crazy to think back to 2000 when James Craig and Gideon Choi instructed me to leave my shining complete in a North Carolina airport parking lot after a Blind tour, explaining it was too burdensome to bring on the plane. I had then only recently got hooked up and didn't want to leave anything behind, but these guys were used to having tons of new stuff so they persuaded me it was right. The tour was a departure from the small filming trips I was used to and I was a rookie filmer among seasoned pros that had been on so many tours they had lost count. Blind had made over a million dollars for Dwindle that year and Ronnie and all the guys were used to the best- I was used to the streets and having to sneak into skate events, so nice hotels, motels and restaurants and participating in the actual event made me feel like it was on. Plus, the skaters I was with were some of the best in the world. They knew all the tricks.

This tour was before the explosion of cell phones and Ronnie bought us all little texting computers to contact each other and our chicks back home. Before we went to the airport we checked out mega-gear from the warehouse in back of Dwindle and stuffed it into our luggage for the trip. Me, James and Gideon smuggled weed to Ohio from LAX; I hid mine in an aspirin canister, which was nothing compared to what James and Gideon brought (over a half ounce), and it had no problem making it through the x-ray scanner. All three of us shared a room and immediately took the smoke alarm battery out.

The Blind skaters were really into gambling and each threw in a $100 bill on the first night of tour and rolled dice to win the pot. They all rolled to see who would go first and Creager got the highest number. He blew on the dice, cupping them in his hand as he shook 'em, then rolled and won straight out. There was a brief pause when the dice stopped, then everyone went crazy! James said "this always happens" and told Ronnie he had the magic touch- even his skating was talked about this way. The guys really looked up to him.

At the very first demo, I really needed to skate from being cramped in the car, plane and hotel, so when I watched the guys starting to warm up on the course I knew I had to skate. Gideon- who was the most stoned out of all the Blind riders- said that I should skate the demos because we were short of riders at the time because Gershon and Josh were caught up on other summer tours, so I did. Ronnie and James started ripping the demo and while I was busy skating, Ronnie did the tallest kickflip back tail from flat on a super tall funbox. I didn't see the trick and it only registered when I heard the crowd roar. James came up to me and said "did you get that back tail?" I felt bad and didn't even have my camera out. The other guys started getting pissed that I wasn't filming and it became a recurring theme throughout the tour, as I was an addict for skating- letting my addiction take control. I thought any real skater would praise me for skating but it was just the opposite. The dudes were bummed. They were hungry for footage and made a clear distinction between filmer and filmed. Ronnie came up to me and nicely tried to break it down that I was responsible for the footage, giving me a little motivation by saying "this is your tour." Seu Trinh was a bit less nice and told me to "give it up" (referring to skating), telling me to be realistic, saying I should only film while the other guys at the table nodded sympathetically like it was best for me. Seu said "look Gayton, James has a trick knee Gideon's ankles are giving, Josh is crazy; we have enough problems, just film."

Ronnie would never be a part of knocking skating and stayed out of the conversation. He was one of the biggest supporters of my skating. I would do little pop shuv-it late flips and he'd always get psyched and remind himself that he had to get his switch ones back. The dude blew the whole worlds mind when he did a switch hardflip late flip over the funbox at Tampa Pro in a 411 video. That's why I always laughed when he complimented my skating. Back home he would always film me if he was done skating or just wasn't feeling it and give me boards and gear, once dumping his entire Droors box (which was enormous) into the back seat of my car. On top of being a skating genius he's what I consider a real pro and sometimes got hammers before eleven a.m. to avoid the heat in the Orange County summers. He's dedicated to practice and sees the world around him strictly as a place to skate, always eyeballing spots from his car and checking out their skateability.

I met him through filming Rodney, who would sometimes borrow his tables to film on the weekends. Ronnie would skate with him when he was shooting once in a while, and after seeing me around a lot he began asking me to film. That resulted in a long string of clips filmed over a few years. I was super into his tricks and was blown away at how naturally talented and blessed by skating he was. He was basically the best skaters I'd ever seen. He could do anything. Moves would just come to him and what he was doing was so far ahead of anything out there that it seemed like he made it up on the spot. All I had to do was hold the camera steady and keep the record button on and everyday would be full of clips. We shot the first backside tail, backside flip ever on film. He did it across a huge third stair ledge and slid for an eternity before flipping out. It became a 411 opener; It took a few years but then all the skaters started doing it. When Ronnie wasn't around, James would tell you some freaky stuff about first try lands, like Ronnie was an alien. He would whisper when he talked about him like it was a big secret, and look out for Ronnie to make sure he wasn't listening. Once during the tour in the hallway of a hotel, Creager asked to see James' board and did a nosewheelie to nollie heel on the carpet first try; handing it back he said "thank you." Everyone just looked at him dumbstruck and he walked into the elevator laughing.

During long stretches in the van James told some comic stories about Robbie Mckinley, a.ka. Robbie Mccrooks. He covered the same ground with him on tour years earlier and was there when he earned the name McCrooks by doing every crooked grind possible at demos: nollie k, fakie k, every kind of switch k, overcrooks, half-cab, everything. James said Robbie would beg girls he brought back to the room for head, asking over and over 'til they finally said yes- James said in his hype voice "and it worked EVERYTIME!" He was the youngest pro on Blind and his excitement for life broke the monotony of endless hours of driving, sometimes in the wrong direction. After one demo a girl latched on to James and came to dinner with us, sitting alone with him while we all bunched up next to a video game watching them stealthily. Gideon called it out when he started kissing her, straining to see with his periphery like a dirty old man, which is what a person becomes after a tour that long. It was a sausage festival in the sports bar- super depressing. James stayed with the girl at the hotel but came into the room while we were all rolling dice and almost bursted when he said, "what's up guys!" Everyone stayed silent and pretended not to hear him, bitter that we couldn't get laid. He was wet from showering and had a huge shit-eating grin on his face, looking around for approval then leaving soon after he made the comment. When he shut the door behind him Gideon said "I hate how James always brags." The next morning when we packed into the van the girl came up and had us autograph magazines for souveniers, having James do it last and giving him a big smooch goodbye. He kept getting texts from her on the rest of the trip and was so sprung he considered coming back to visit when the trip was over.

The highlight of the tour was the Flushing Meadows pool Jason Dill skated in *Trilogy*. There are marble ledges over grates all around the circumference and the grates extended out like spokes on a wheel around the entire place, ending in the center where there's a huge metal globe sculpture. It was the perfect summer day and the place was packed with people. I must've changed out three tapes trying to keep up with the skaters who were doing all kinds of tricks over the gaps and ledges. I filmed clips of Ronnie on the ledge over gap that ended up in ES shoes' *Menikmati* and he was skating so much that day that a rogue filmer had to pick up the slack (the dude was shady though and Ronnie never retrieved the footage). Even though James was recovering from a bad knee injury, he never held back, skating all the spots. He filmed a varial heel over the grate then did a front krook to fakie on one of the tall, granite ledges. Gideon did the sickest gap to front blunt from a ledge on top into the pool. The ground is so smooth that I wanted to skate the spot badly as I filmed, but so much was going down that I forgot about it and never got a chance to skate. I can't remember if the sun came out and then it got cloudy, but it was overcast when I was filming James and then blazing hot and humid the rest of the day. We saw Rodney Torres hanging out with no board just watching the skating, and Pelon from the Inland Empire in Cali who did a mega long blindside frontside noseslide on the ledge over grate.

Josh Kasper grabbed me to film a gigantic ollie on a set of stairs in the back where he had to jump off immediately to avoid a network of emptied pools when he made it. He took his time in between tries and skated hella fast to make it over the enormous steps that seemed to be made for a giant. Josh was wearing a leather Harley Davidson hat strap thing which kept his hair back- he was crazy like that. He also thought he was The Rock. His skating was different than the other guys because each trick was an insane stunt that usually ended in failure, (only because it was always such a huge gamble), while most of the Blind riders were focused on ledges, popped flips and consistency.

Gershon was on the trip and he was the first to suggest a rain skate at the last demo, which was at an all masonite park. There were pools of water everywhere. I filmed him do the fattest caught and turned backside flip on a steep bank that was soaking wet, then go across to the next bank and 360 flip to fakie. On another day in Pennsylvania he crooked a flat bar, then popped over to frontside krook on the other side; I was zoomed in so close that the sweat could be seen visibly flying from his pants in the 100 plus degree weather. That night Gershon rinsed his clothes in the bath and hung them on the shower curtain so they wouldn't get ruined. I went through about three shirts that day. To save them, I tried drying them on the van when we stopped at a restaurant after the demo. They were all laid out on the top and back when James came up and convinced me to throw them out- shaking his head and blinking his eyes compassionately he looked at me like it wasn't worth it.

In Boston we ran into Tobias Keith (a former Transworld photographer) who showed us some spots and invited us to his house where some of the photos he'd shot over the years were hanging up. One was of a front blunt on a ledge lit up with so many strobes that it created multiple copies of the skater in alternate universes. He had an impressive book collection and really was into Hunter S. Thompson, telling us about some of his work. Not too long ago I watched a documentary on Hunter. In it he talked about typing out literary classics so he could feel what it was like to write a great book. When I talked about Henry Miller he cut me off and told me about a passage in a Hunter novel where Hunter changes the subject from a string of thoughts to "…fuck this! I'm gonna go get some coke." To him that was cutting edge writing and he didn't want to hear anything about Miller.

He took us to a gap that dropped from the sidewalk above over a grass slope landing into a school playground. Mark Nichols was getting a third angle long lens while the team manager and myself stood ready, both with fish eye. I switched sides at the last second because I had trouble with the angle and was too far away when he landed it the next try. He was disgusted by the shot and said, "throw that angle in the trash!" Between three filmers not one angle was viable, and Mark's shot turned out reddish orange. Josh tried to redo it but cracked his board and got hurt too many times, screaming abuses and asking the stars above, "why?!" He gave up on the gap and tried a few lines inside the schoolyard that were pretty sick, but he didn't get 'em and we ended up leaving.

Boston had the best weed of the whole tour; James even commented that it was the best weed he'd ever got on any tour. Most of the herb for sale in the Midwest and on the East Coast is dirt weed that's brown or faded green and loaded with seeds. If you ask for chronic, the people selling the crap will advise you that it's 'all your gonna find around here' (mostly true). We had made plans to pick up some good herb from a friend of a friend and I had to rush Josh who was trying casper stalls on some historic looking marble. He didn't smoke so it annoyed him that we were in such a hurry. The guy selling the weed was leaving for work soon on the night shift and we were gonna miss him if we didn't take off fast; plus we hardly knew how to get there. Somehow, I got everyone in the tour van rolling to the dude's house. He was almost out the door when we met up with him, thinking we weren't coming, and he quickly weighed us out a half ounce of the most crystallized, dank smelling weed one could hope to find on the road, for $180. James gave me more than enough for his and Gideon's share and the two of them couldn't stop talking about the weed being the best they'd ever got on the road. After getting back we smoked in the room with the windows open and began making fun of Josh who was next door and a welcome target for criticism because everything he said came off as arrogant, insulting or fantasy prone. When he arrived on tour I somehow ended up in the van with him after the other guys went to check into the hotel. He asked questions about the tour and demanded a sort of update like he was CEO of the team, which was hilarious because the other riders wanted nothing more than to see him booted off Blind. Josh's dramatic, over-the-top personality was hilarious to James and the guys and an unlimited source of entertainment during tour downtime. I remember Gideon looking over at Josh stretching in the middle of the course before a demo and say, "there goes Josh, building the drama."

After a few joints I started getting paranoid about talking so much shit when I realized he might be able to hear us in the next room because both our windows were open. I told James this and he replied, "Josh *knows* we talk shit about him," which made everyone burst out laughing. There were ads for his Osiris shoe that showed him on one side looking like The Rock, lifting one eyebrow in the photo and challenging Kanten Russel, who was pictured next to him, with the wording "I'm going to put the smack down on his candy ass!" All joking aside though, Josh did big shit that drew in crowds; he closed one demo with an immense tre-flip over a super-sized funbox *and* a large crowd of kids on the other side. All the other dudes could say after something like that was, 'damn!' They had respect for his skating and never said anything negative about it except to point out that his frontside flips were pop shuv-its (illusion flips).

Nobody was immune to the shit talking the Blind team did. Anyone who left the room came under the microscope, and they weren't above lying to enhance the gossip or to cover up insane pranks. The whole day was filled with trickery around them and they never got bored of it. Seu told me that Creager, on an old tour, stole his undeveloped film rolls containing the flicks for an entire trip and pulled the film out of the rolls like string, exposing them all! Seu blew a transistor in his brain and started freaking out, totally letting it get to him and almost having a nervous breakdown before Ronnie produced the real film and told Seu the others were blank rolls- it was Seu's initiation.

The humidity in and around the East Coast is unbearable in the summer, and the three-week tour was memorable for sweat, uncomfortable cots and an on the positive side some of the best skating I'll probably ever see. There was supposed to be an article in Transworld about the trip that Seu compiled photos for and the editors even scanned in, but Ronnie forgot to turn in the text- so an entire article worth of photos were never published, including a flick I got in Pennsylvania. He had his reasons for not turning it in (that no one will ever know), and it was in all probability as mysterious as the fact that only one side of the moon faces us at all times, while we get dizzy spinning.

Gideon would call Ronnie a skate rat, referring to how much he actually skated, and it made me think of the Inglewood Skate Rats (IWSR). I always thought of where they were now and how unbelievable it would be if they knew how far I'd gotten in skating; that I was being flown around and had free gear to burn. But no matter where I go, how much free stuff I get or what tricks I land, it still doesn't match that original feeling I had in the streets and in pools, when skating was brand new to me and I felt the pull of its addiction. Everybody that skates seriously had a similar group of friends, and the sad thing is usually only one guy out of an entire group of skaters ends up sticking with it- if that. I've heard these same stats from Ron Chatman and the funny thing is a lot of pros have told me that the guys they grew up skating with were way better than they *ever* were. A common thing I hear is "if he only kept skating…" Once after a long day of filming, Ronnie broke out some old 8mm and Hi-8 tapes from before he was sponsored where him, Heath Kirchart and Ryan Ellis were filming each other, circa 1990. Seeing them made me understand a comment he made on tour when we were on the East Coast. It was at night when we were in the van at a gas station, and over to the left were mini manual pads that he said looked like a place he used to skate 'til two in the morning when he was younger- one of the spots on the tapes fit that description exactly. On this old tape he showed me, Ronnie and his friends were filming each other with no regard for distance or framing, just firing from the hip. In one section of night footage the cameraman called a local chick over that was passing by and kept filming while he was talking to her- even when Ronnie landed a bunch of tricks in a row- only briefly pausing to yell out, "go ron!" The footage was orange from the streetlights and hardly discernable from focus blur, but it had heart and was a classic snapshot in time of probably the most fun all those guys ever had skating, including Ronnie.

His other passion is remote control cars that he builds himself to run around tracks made specifically for r/c or in dirt fields that have biker jumps. It's been years since I've talked to him. I think the last time I saw him was at the Blind premier. Just yesterday I saw a man jumping a huge remote control dune buggy over a set of dirt moguls in the grounds of Harbor City Lake, formerly the home of Reggie the Alligator who the bus driver mentioned as we passed the lake going up PCH. I was coming back from Transitions Skate Shop where I just got a new board and wheels that I badly needed. The owner took real care in setting up my deck and oiled my bearings and replaced any missing bolts for free as he put it together like a true adept. The walls and ceiling are covered with old boards and posters (one of Rosa naked in a pile of *Shorty's* bolts) that put you in a skate frame of mind; and for people like myself, that witnessed the evolution of skate shapes, brings it all back to when nothing mattered in life but what deck you had or which one you wanted to get. As I was leaving he gave me the new Transworld for the ride home. In it was a Wes Kramer pro spotlight and a cover shot of him doing a darkslide down a rail. In the article they only mentioned Rodney's name third or fourth as one of the originators of the darkslide when he's the only one to ever really explore the trick and create different versions of it that no one can touch. One variation that I filmed of his was across two long skate boxes about two foot off the ground, where he nosewheelied to nollie half cab heel across the gap to darkslide on the second box. Danny Garcia was there and the funny thing is that after a conversation the two of them had in between Rodney skating, he landed the trick *first try*, like a miracle. It was almost like the rest did some good and allowed Rodney to clear his mind and forget that he couldn't do it. I was shitting bricks when he landed it because it was unexpected and my little one-chip camera had no room for error through such a small aperture. Some of the tries I was reviewing were missing his board completely, so I had no idea how this one turned out. After everyone in the park congratulated him he came over to me asking to see the shot and it was like the moment of truth playing the clip, which came out perfect. I acted like I knew it would. Somehow I always got lucky with Rod's tricks (like his handstand, fingerflip to nosemanual). I've heard nightmare stories from other filmers about missing clips of his because they weren't paying attention. The nature of Rodney's tricks, being so original, automatically constitutes a certain length of time involved in conjuring something new out of thin air. He's making it up as he goes along, but once he lands one, the others just roll out. This was the case with backside flip darkslides. He had been asking me if I knew any spots that would be good for the trick so I brought him to a ledge on Catalina Landing in Long Beach to film the trick. I always used to skate it with my crew back in the day and I knew the top of the ledge had more than enough space for a darkslide. I first brought him to Bum Park but I think a homeless person was sprawled across the ledge, so he decided to try it at Catalina Landing where he made it like magic within an hour. It was like having luck fishing when he landed the backside darkslide, and he popped out 180 on instinct; plus, the trick was so futuristic that it gave the morning a new feeling and we were both buzzed from the make. A kid coming off the Catalina Express recognized Rodney and told me with starry eyes that he wished it was his job to film him and that I didn't know how lucky I was. Looking down at my clothes and feeling a rumbling in my tummy from no food made me look at him funny. Rodney gave him an autograph and sent him on his way to begin trying a few more darkslides when a bicycle cop rolled up and told us to leave. The next day he went back to Bum Park with a different filmer and Socrates taking photos, landing the trick three or four more times on an even thinner, higher ledge. The one I shot ended up in a Tensor Trucks ad as a video sequence turned into a magazine ad. I still have a copy of it folded up somewhere. I used to be psyched on all the stuff I shot and tried to collect it.

The bus I took on the way back from Transitions goes right to the Long Beach Transit Mall in the other direction, skating distance from Catalina Landing and Bum Park where I used to skate all the time and chased out by cops almost every time. As the bus passed into Harbor City a short, sort of stunted elderly man got on the bus holding a bag of change and wobbling around, unable to hold his balance on the quickly moving bus. He had on a Sunday suit and was smiling the whole time underneath his huge glasses with such a humility that I wanted to imitate him and I think a smile came across my face. There's less isolation, socially, riding the bus as opposed to a car. On the bus you're riding with everybody like one big family. That's why skating around a city is so cool, you get to see everything. The best spots are always the most abandoned areas like Santa Fe Street in South Central, which has amazing spots but is a shady area. I would always be amazed that someone like Rodney would see a run down place in the armpit of L.A. as a golden opportunity for footage. When I filmed him he'd always carry a few five-dollar bills in his pocket for the occasional homeless person asking for change and a lot of times I would have to pause filming because Rodney would be so interested in their story that he'd get caught up talking to them and forget he was skating. Some of the homeless people were less coherent and sort of scary, but in such a bad state that you only had to push slowly to avoid them. Once a crazed addict came up to us on Santa

Fe in South Central showing us his heroin sac, asking if we wanted to do any with a fading smile on his face that flashed into a paranoid expression then back to a crazy grin again. He walked away after we ignored him, then turned around and came back asking if he could borrow my board and that we should all skate to Venice. After a few more times walking away and coming back he vanished into the filthy background, but for a minute it seemed like he wasn't going to leave.

I've heard of people being robbed for their VX1000s around South Central at gunpoint and also at the L.A. Convention Center where I felt sketched out a few times myself, once filming Marc Johnson where a burly Samoan stared at us from a bike with a sour look on his face the entire time we filmed, like he couldn't stand to see us skating. Luckily that day we got the trick in eleven tries and the guy faded away even before that, to go mad dog someone else probably. When we first got there, Marc set up a board and explained to me that with all the responsibility involved with Enjoi he hadn't skated in a few weeks, which was such a smokescreen, that for a second I lost confidence in the day. The trick was a manual to 360 flip manual again across the brown marble gap at the L.A. Convention Center. He ran up the stairs to get speed and jump on his board, having barely any room for set up, and manual tre-flipped manual with perfect form (I was filming for Enjoi but it ended up in *Yeah Right*). When he ollied off the stairs on the other side he rolled in an arc back towards me and said, "that was a freak of nature," referring to how fast he got the trick. After watching it a few times he packed up and left. He said he'd buy me lunch because he was so hyped on the clip, but I said no thanks and that I needed to get back to my girl whom I was obsessed with at the time. He understood but could tell she was making me a little crazy because she kept calling the whole time we filmed. I ended up having my first kid with her and she almost succeeded in driving me nuts before we split up and made it to where I couldn't film as much.

At the time I was making a video called Crouching Filmer, Hidden Poacher that contained an amazing first ever part of Justin Eldridge and also Clark Hassler. Daniel Lebron, Jesus Fernandez and Alfonso Fernandez shared a part and didn't even know the video had been released (that's how underground it was) when my friend Brandon Manzaneras gave Lebron a copy when he was visiting from Spain. It was only released on VHS because Dwindle decided not to back it after it was complete (even after advertising it at the

Long Beach trade show in their booth), and I could only afford tapes when I self-released it. That one of the Spaniards received it in the end and brought it back to Barcelona made all the editing and headaches worthwhile. It actually made me feel like I could retire because these guys were inspiring everyone in L.A. when they lived here and for Lebron to have gotten copy after the final edit felt like completion but ran in line with all the other odd coincidences and lucky occurrences throughout my life.

The Spaniards (that's what everyone in L.A. called them) were legendary at the USC blocks before and after 2000. I remember the distinct smack of the nose hitting the block on a halfcab flip noseslide and seeing Jesus Fernandez roll away fakie with a big *yahhhhhhhh* from all the local skaters. They were always landing amazing shit.

You couldn't go there without seeing them, so of course they were the ones getting rolled all the time. I remember a cop letting him go after shredding his wrist with handcuffs for skating the blocks. He would've taken him to jail if he didn't see blood. USC was a huge bust. When they took the cuffs off he said, "I'll be back tomorrow," right to their face with a smile as Daniel sat waiting for him. They were here in L.A. for a few years but stayed way passed their visa dates and eventually had to leave their South Central apartment and go back to Spain; not before thoroughly killing it though (they also burned it with chicks at USC; they left broken hearts and I think a few babies behind) Their place just up the street from blocks was a classic skate pad with mags everywhere, a bong on the table and a skate vid playing on the T.V. at all times. When I first visited there Lebron showed me a seeded up weed plant growing in his closet that he was very proud of. It was about four and a half foot tall and growing under what looked like a regular household lightbulb. He also showed me a bunch of artwork his father had drawn mostly with Jesus as the subject, saying to me "my father likes very much Jesus Christ." They also sat around playing a nylon string guitar as they watched skate videos in between sessions at SC. Daniel could play classic Spanish guitar songs and sing at the same time. The Spaniards didn't try to adapt to American culture- they kept it real and influenced us with their lifestyle. They all rode for Neighborhood Skates (run by Julio De La Cruz), and I would always see ads with them all over Transworld with stylish photos and creative layouts. Jesus was the only one to go pro out of the three and his parts in the Chocolate and Girl videos probably made all the people who saw them skating USC back in the day reminisce about the era.

It seems like I've driven to hell and back on the L.A. freeways with so many near misses in traffic that the bus seems like a safer bet any day. I can't help but reflect on the bus rides I take and all my thoughts revolve around skating. I switch tailslid the window with my fingers and ollie out above the frame like it's a vert ramp. I can't focus on anything serious, all my thoughts just revert to skating. The headaches associated with having a car are enough without the danger of driving one and if it wasn't enough taking skaters to every spot the L.A. freeways extend, I also was the main driver on most tours I filmed, trying to apply Los Angeles style driving to the Midwest and Canada. Once I got two van loads of skaters pulled over by a Mounty that was more concerned about our driving than the ticket he was giving us. We were speeding and he asked us please to slow down, and couldn't understand why anyone would drive us, with a real look of concern on his face. Compared to Canadian drivers, us Angelinos probably seemed like maniacs, and we were. The ticket haunted me until my mom moved and they had no address to send it to, although they are probably still trying. Eventually I'll have to pay it if I want to go back. Having been raised in L.A. the contrast in culture is so great it might as well be the other side of the world; and being there made me question where I was raised, like it was a bad environment for a child to grow in, although perfect for skating. If one could put up with the smog, the heavy traffic, the filthy streets, the crazy people and the general busy feel of the city, and you've never known anything else, it might seem perfect. But one visit to a place like Canada would immediately warp that perception. It was almost the complete antithesis of L.A. The people are so cool that it seems like a different dimension where almost nothing bad happens- an America that hasn't been spoiled, except that they have crazy winters that go on forever, making it unbearable. A chick teased me in Vancouver while I was drunk one night standing in line trying to get pizza somewhere, saying that Canadian women give better head because of the long winters- probably true. When my son was born a nurse remarked the same thing about couples getting snuggly in the winter, using each other's bodies for heat and babies popping out around summer as a result.

Canadian skaters are some of the coolest people I've ever met. Going on tour there made me feel the love that I'd heard about (like some fantasy 'cuz I'm from the dirty ass streets) from Corey Shepherd and Chris Haslam. Vancouver had a huge skate scene and it just so happened that we were gonna be there for the premier of the first ever *Red Dragons* video.

I found out about the trip on short notice and I had maybe two days to get ready because the other filmer backed out. The TM hit me up while I was still in my chonies and I threw all kinds of clothes and boards and shit together and made sure I had a grip of blank tapes to burn. Soc gave me two boxes of tapes for two weeks. The tour began super shitty with me waiting at the airport for six hours with the Dwindle team manager, pacing back and forth for the arrival of Gailea Momolu and Marcus McBride who's planes were coming from different parts of the U.S. I almost went insane from the boredom and my stomach was grumbling from not eating. We were in an empty part of the Chicago Airport with hardly any windows and it was like being in prison having to wait that long. The TM didn't seem to mind almost like he was used to it from the shitty planning on these tours, and he kept laughing at how impatient I was getting. When we finally got to Canada and were going through customs I was asked the purpose of my visit and I replied "working, filming skateboarding". The woman looked at me with her mouth open, just super pissed and had to walk away to ask her boss something, making me crap my pants and feel ultra-paranoid that I might be flying back the same day I came in. I had no idea what I could've done wrong. When she left to talk to her supervisor the TM looked at me crazy and said "you weren't supposed to say that"; but I'd never been filming out of the country and he hadn't told me what to say at all. What a dick. She came back and gave me a bunch of shit about how I should have a work permit and that a Canadian should be doing the job, not a foreigner. She let us go but flagged us so that the customs guards searched our gear. They found a medical hash lollipop wrapper and said, "you got any drugs on ya buddy." I said no and that it wasn't even mine. They asked me to identify some new Ventures in my bag and then let me go. J.B. Gillet, who was arriving from France, got strip searched down to his Polo boxers. He was cleverly hiding the dankest ball of hashish under his nut sack. It was a little smaller than a ping pong ball and lasted almost the entire trip, though he mixed it with mostly tobacco, but whatever- the hash smelled like Super Skunk and was similar to putty the quality was so good. To boot, Canadians have excellent weed and Marcus, having been to Canada many times riding for 101, told me that we should expect to see some real dank once we got closer to Vancouver. I swear, the nerdiest guys you ever saw smoked us out after one demo and I don't know if it was because I had just skated, but the weed made my legs go numb as we drove the van away. It was super creeper and I didn't realize how powerful it was 'til we got back to the hotel. I quickly made sure I still had their number in my pocket, frantically checking (super stoned at this point), and almost panicked that I lost it which made everyone bust up laughing. What a rookie. It was the best weed I had ever smoked.

It was Chris Haslam's first tour. Back then he didn't look anything like the Haslam we all know and love- he was clean shaven and hadn't found his style yet. The tricks were all there though and Chris busted at the first demo with Marcus, J.B., Gailea, Aaron Snyder and Louie Barletta. It was a mixture of teams on what Dwindle termed a super tour, which had been going on a few weeks; I had just jumped on the last leg. It was the first tour where I felt like I was doing my job properly, getting all the tricks and communicating with the skaters to get all the footage I could. Marcus was always coming through and at night he would ask me to see the footage, which I transferred onto a master tape after each demo. He's seriously the coolest people on Earth and is one of the best skaters in the world- a seasoned vet. But it's beyond that, his skating is something that has to be witnessed in person to really grasp what a pro skater should be. The kids at the demos would be transfixed on him. I guess that many years touring and skating demos taught him how to excite the crowd.

He was always in the zone, skating with his earphones on as he blasted huge kickflips out of banks that swiveled in slow motion before they sucked up to his feet. When he watched his footage at night it was usually with a spliff in his hand while listening to music, rewinding it over and over, even watching the other guys tricks in slow mo. He remembered every shot and when I saw him later at the Santa Monica Courthouse with Stevie, he told me I forgot the nollie heel at the first demo on the final edit- what a great memory.

  I shared a room with Marcus and J.B. pretty much the whole trip. In one hotel the other skaters were staying in the room next to us and we opened the adjoining doors and combined the rooms so it was one big one.   J.B. really made me feel comfortable on this tour and he called me crazy when he put his earphones on my head because I always laughed when I hung out with him. Everything he said with his French accent was funny to me. I flipped out at how dope the beat and Lyrics were on the Lunatic album (rapping in French). He then handed me the spliff and let me listen to the rest, but I kept rewinding the same part of the song on the portable cd player like Marcus rewinding the tricks- it was too good. J.B. explained what the rapper was saying and it was so sick- I could hardly make out the basics, even though I took French in college but I felt like I was experiencing the evolution of music and I didn't even have to know what they were saying- the French language alone is like music. Marcus showed me how to rinse my clothes and keep them fresh after a demo by hanging them over the shower curtain rod to dry. He skated in sports gear he had bought and wasn't about to lose his investment. I was the filmer and had to preserve what little clothes I got from the company in contrast to the healthy boxes sponsored skaters were allotted, so it was a welcome lesson. He's mostly quiet and I interpreted this as him being so psyched on his life and his skating, that there was just the sickest beat playing in his head with or without headphones on and words would just ruin the vibe.

It was August 2001 and the tour ended sixteen days before 911. We probably would've had serious problems getting into Canada if the tour happened after the Twin Towers fell. The first demo was in Edmonton and the last was in Vancouver. Every spot we skated had been featured in the tour sections of various company videos I had seen and even some of the guest clips of locals were identical. Haslam did the sickest darkslide in Calgary going down a long, kinked ledge to fakie. Haslam was so dedicated at the time. At demos he would bust the most amazing shit. I feel bad too because I'd be so hung over, or just lazy, and he'd knock at my door early in the morning asking if I wanted to go skate (just to give you a clue about how much he actually skated). I told him I'd go a few times but I could never make the 7 or 8 a.m. skate he was used to. That was me a few years earlier, but now I was a scumbag. I watched him grow as a skater -going back and forth from Canada to L.A.- and the bag of tricks and originality just blossomed. When he came into his own it was gnarly to watch him because the bar kept rising and he was always on the attack. Daewon would trip out on Haslam and he turned him pro quick. Everyone was like "what the fuck, this dudes from another planet." Like Tony Mag, "he did it all, everything, everything, every, every, everything." Gailea was also ripping at the demo and nollie half cab heel lipslid down steep rails and flat bars. He was young and thirsty so one night I took him to a club and the bouncer out front freaked out about my California I.D. He yelled to the crowd, "hey, this guy is from California!"

Everyone cheered and patted my back on the way in- we must've been in the sticks. Like I said, Canada is another dimension compared to L.A. Inside we had a few drinks and tried to talk to some girls that weren't having it. Gailea heard his song and said, "this is my jam," floating into the crowd and pumping his fists wearing a white sweatband around his head and on his wrists just vibrating with the song. Afterward we went to meet the Canadian kids with the good weed. We stopped near a park in a rural suburb and smoked out in the open. They explained to us that having one or two plants in Canada is normal and that the police don't bug people about smoking. They told me I would move there someday and had no doubt in their mind that I eventually would, confidently nodding yes while at the same time squinting their eyes.

When we got to Calgary there were fires and the smoke got caught in between the tall buildings lining the street our hotel was on which made it hazy and ashes were falling from the sky. The meals were comped and I ate the best maple glazed salmon again and again in the hotel restaurant, closing my eyes to savor the bites it was so tasty (and even asked my girl to try and make it once I got back to L.A; it couldn't be duplicated). After a few demos in Calgary we drove towards the west coast seeing the dormant ski jumps at the top of mountain peaks that were waiting for the snow. We drove for hours and saw nothing but dense forest that was so immense and seemingly unlimited. I told J.B. that Bigfoot definitely lived there. The countryside was immense and gave me a good idea of how vast and open our world actually is. Some of the rivers were sky blue, unreal like something only a computer could create and everywhere I looked a tiny piece of heaven appeared. I felt stupid for just passing through and not stopping to enjoy it a little but we had to keep on schedule. We went from Edmonton and Red Deer to Calgary, Kelowna and Abbotsford before we reached the end of the line, Vancouver. Here we found the best weed of the tour and it wasn't even dry yet. Marcus told me, "this is the stuff I was talking about," but pointed out that it was still a little wet.

The Vancouver demo was termed *casual,* which meant the pros didn't really skate, because they didn't have to and they were beat. I took advantage and got out all the energy I had balled up from only filming for the past week and a half by skating the demo. Moses Itkonen had a lot of footage at this park and he gets mega credit as it was gnarly and the hits spit me out more than a few times. I was drenched by the time I was done- every shred of clothing was wet and my shoes were bubbling and squishing while I walked. Haslam was psyched on a nosegrind I did down a hubba and commented (mercifully) that he had never seen anyone do it. After the guys signed a few autographs we took off. At a gas station when Marcus and I were in the van and everyone had gone inside the mini-mart, he busted the fattest freestyle that I couldn't even remember if I was under regressive hypnosis but can only tell you it was perfect and somehow incorporated sticking his dick in his girl.

When we all settled into the rooms we began trying to smoke a half-ounce before the next morning, as we obviously couldn't bring it on the plane. Louie Barletta left right away in a cab to get Absynthe, which is legal in Vancouver. The next morning a pile of puke about two feet high attested to how powerful it was. Louie was super creative skating and I remember him doing fingerflips to switch nosemanual, fakie flip out as well as ripping the living shit out of a mini ramp during a demo. I saw a few sequences that Seu shot from the earlier portion of the tour, and one was of Louie doing a blindside flip to front board down a rail. That night Louie bursted into our room and snatched a few beers, then vanished after mumbling a few unintelligible words. J.B. shook his head saying that it wasn't cool for him to do that. It was either the beer or the spliffs J.B. kept rolling, but I ended up puking. It was toward the end of the night and we had tried our damndest to smoke as much as we could when suddenly my face turned blue and I started rocking back and forth as J.B. made fun of me saying, "what's the matter you can't *handle it*!" He laughed uncontrollably as I ran to the toilet. I had told him how cholos in L.A. said *handle it* as a way of saying 'do it' and he couldn't get enough of it, playing the phrase out the whole tour along with adding *meeeaaaaaan* to the front of every noun. We had to leave a bunch of the weed for the maids as we had to get on a plane the next morning, so it was a tragedy. I said a little prayer for it. We took a team picture for a Canadian skate mag before we left the hotel, then loaded up and bounced. There were so many taxes and fees at the airport and in order to get back to L.A. I had to run and bug the Team Manager for extra Canadian ends. He was tired of me asking for shit. I slept almost the entire plane flight back and when we arrived at L.A.X., Aaron Snyder summed up the entire tour in a phrase and said, "Canada, we *handled it*."

Only a week after we got back a few of us felt the need to recapture the flame of the Canadian tour and Seu Trinh and I organized a trip to S.F. to link up with Marcus. We dug up as many skaters as we could, including Gailea, and rented a van to go film and shoot photos. Clark Hassler came with us on what turned out to be a week-long trip that Ronnie Creager joined midway through. Tony (the team manager) came to handle the finances and get second angle. He is the coolest guy and if you ever read this buddy, thank you for all the boxes, I know I bugged you a grip.

Seu was always out for photos and would sometimes ask skaters to do tricks on a certain obstacle because he could see the photo potential. He wouldn't be picky about the tricks, he just asked if someone wanted to skate it and sometimes he would ask me if I had anything (he'd say "get up there Gayton"). When he pointed out a rail into dirt on the side of the road somewhere around the grapevine, I ended up being the only one who did anything. I cavemanned the rail and kept getting stuck in the dirt on the landing. Gailea seemed irritated that I was taking so long and kept telling me to bend my legs. I rolled away the next try. Seu got two angles with an ultra expensive Hasablat camera that had an equally expensive lens.

That night we made it to S.F. and checked into the hotel where I began rolling a huge joint with *Mike Tyson* weed and hash oil dripped inside. (Way after the trip I actually saw Mike Tyson buying weed at a medical clinic- when I left I saw the hugest crowd of people surrounding him at his Blue Bentley parked on La Brea). Seu and I wanted to go out so we headed to a club first thing and left the youngsters behind, as they were under age. We got stupid and Seu ended up talking to a girl, calling her peaches and ignoring her real name even though she kept correcting him over and over. He was drunk and showed her a Polaroid of me skating that day explaining, "*this* is the skater- *I'm* the photographer!" She wasn't impressed and just laughed in his face but that didn't stop him. He ended up jumping on her hood and denting it as she tried to leave afterward and yelling PEACHES! over and over as I peeled him off the car. After that night he told me I was certified. That was a turning point for him and when we got back home he grew his hair long, went crazy and became a total chick magnet; but his photography never suffered.

The next day we went to SLAP. Seu wanted to visit Mark Whitley and see what's up with running an article about our trip. I immediately began talking to a girl who was doing graphic design in the office. We started a conversation about chapstick somehow. I pointed out that it becomes addicting. If you run out your lips are so used to it they dry up, and she said "yah look at how many I have," showing me about five different ones. We talked about a few other things then I asked her if she wanted to go to a bar that night, and she was down. She knew about a spot in North Beach and after we picked Ronnie up from the airport and got him settled at the hotel, a few of us headed out to meet her. I forget her name but she brought her roommate out who Seu talked to and, ironically, got a photo published sitting next to at the bar that his girlfriend at the time questioned him about. We drank Negro Modelos and spent a bunch of money on the juke box closing the place down and taking a cab back to her place. The cab was taking too long so I kissed her up against the wall and everyone tried to make us feel uncomfortable. Seu didn't hit it off with her roommate so Creager joined us and had the girls laughing the rest of the night, making strange observations. He said the funniest shit nonstop and the girls busting up so much made me kind of realize how funny he was myself. I could see he got the green light and totally could've stayed but ended up getting a cab. He probably wanted to rest up to film the next day (which is when he got his bangers). We drank a few more beers, and when her roommate went to bed we made out in her room (which had a super dim red light glowing in the corner) until the early morning in a haze that felt drug like. I tried several times to have sex with her but she wouldn't let me and we eventually passed out. After waking up we sat around talking in our underwear and listened to music as I rolled a joint of some stale old weed she had in her dresser drawer (stale weed in SF is still insanely potent). It must've been an hour of talking before I had to go to the bathroom and discovered that somehow during the night I had shit my pants bad. Now either she was too nice to mention it or she really didn't notice, but I was laying on my belly the whole time and she claimed not to smell it or see it. She must've had bad eyesight because when I looked at the boxers after I sat on the toilet there was the biggest brown circle seeping through them, pretty much covering my whole butt and I was laying on my belly most of the time we talked. That shows how out of it I was the whole morning, just full of myself and talking too much, because I didn't notice a thing 'til I got to the restroom. I had already thrown the boxers away and showered before I told her. Somehow, after making her laugh about my story, we ended up taking a shower together and making out like crazy just short of me penetrating her. Our lips were raw from kissing. After this we said goodbye and made plans to hang out again that night. I met the guys down in the van after vectoring them to her apartment. They were amazed that I didn't have sex with her, Gailea especially, asking me about ten times to confirm that I didn't and finally accepting it with a "*damnnnnnn.*"

We ended up at Third and Army and right away a bird shit on Gaelia. Mark Whitley came along and Creager somehow mentioned in front of him that I was married (a burn that I deserved) which of course got back to the girl I stayed the night with because it was Mark's co-worker. That's Blind Team initiation shit. Everybody started filming and Ronnie pushed me to shoot a back tail I was doing around the horseshoe ledge that he filmed sick from between the railing on the inside. We drove around to other spots and Ron ended up liking the ledge over double set across from Pier 7 in the newly built plaza. With Seu shooting next to me he did the cleanest front tail 270 down it. It came out amazing and Ronnie gave me a pat on the back just above my butt like football players. Next he went to skate Pier 7 and filmed a fakie flip to fakie manual up the big side, also getting the photo sequence. We filmed some rolling shots and he landed on a switch heel, switch nose manny to fakie double flip that shot out from under him. Later, or the next day, Marcus came down and filmed and photographed a meaty switch backside flip over the pier block. I was right next to Seu shooting and two girls walked in front of my camera just as Marcus did it. Seu was a few feet to the right and his shot wasn't affected (the girls walking by made his sequence look artsy and Strength Magazine ran it soon after). Tony (the TM) got the second angle with my one chip camera and it looked way bigger from the deep side of the block, and also faster 'cuz he struggled to keep

Marcus in frame. These were about the only photos we got on the trip and Seu's idea for an article was never realized.

That night we went to Ameoba and out to eat where we met the girls again. It was the last night we were in town. and after hanging around Haight street for a while we drove the girls home. The Deltron album was playing and everybody in the van, including the girls, knew the lyrics and we all sang along driving through Frisco feeling good vibes. On the way out the next day Clark frontside flipped a popular bump over bar in the Tenderloin (after the spot blew up Josh Kalis did a heelflip body-varial over it). When we pulled up the spot a black dude in a silver Mercedez started his car and drove by and someone saw a woman giving him head. That was the last stop and we headed back to L.A. midday, all scraped up and beat and got to

Dwindle just after dark, then everyone went their separate ways.

9

I feel like I got away with a crime the way I was able to travel skating- I'm just a dirty Skate Rat from Inglewood. Looking at my gear I almost don't believe it myself. My daughter makes fun of the sweat marks on my hat and is more concerned for my welfare than I am. Like I said before, I have one pair of pants, one shirt, one hat and a bunch of mismatched socks- a rich man in some countries. In my backyard the dragonflies are here and spring is turning into summer with the heat making itself known, causing termites to come out of the woodwork by the thousands, flying all over the inside of the house and a few crawling across my pillow, so I guess I'll get up. I was told to leave by my landlord so all the plants and trees I cultivated in my backyard are healthy and vibrant for the next tenants. I'm surprised it took him this long, I haven't paid the rent in months. I took off to Channel Street Skatepark because it's closer to my house than Wilmington. To get there today I had to walk most of the way down Gaffey because the sidewalk is absent along the whole street. I rolled up and nobody was skating; just a few dudes drinking in the parking lot (it sucks skating Channel by yourself but I did anyways, hitting the bowls and the rugged street course). The plaque on one of the walls explained that at first the city was at odds with the construction, but eventually relented and the park became a community mainstay. On the far end another plaque reads that professional photo shoots are by appointment only-

whack! Just twenty feet away from the second plaque is a cell phone tower that looks like a palm tree incognito. The tower made the side of my face buzz and I felt like my thoughts were being scrambled, ruining my meditation and driving me off like a bug deterrent. I walked way up the hill to Western Ave. and began to get disgusted by the city and how we're all packed in like cattle, thinking this while car after car beamed their lights in my face cruising down the hill- I feel helpless and out of place like using the sidewalk is only something prehistoric men do. Somehow though, I can see that this is just a dark corridor, and that these few miles are just the doldrums, the horse latitudes where you jettison all unnecessary weight in order to sail on to the intended destination.

It got really dark when I came to the cemetery on Western and I heard thousands of frogs croaking from the abandoned Navy base across the street. I knew if I stared too long I'd see a fetch loose from it's grave, so I looked straight ahead walking up and over the hill. I wanted to sleep good and I know something creepy like that would keep me up all night.

The miracle of skating is that it evolved out of a concrete world, and even if there is no one around, save for a ghost, the sidewalk is continuous. It almost seems like a skater could ride around the world- street to street, curb to curb; across bridges, through alleys, along the coast, through suburbs and ghettos and valleys- but that's impossible. What I do know is that the beautifully polished concrete on the strand in Hermosa leads all the way to Venice and beyond. If your wheels held out and you had the strength, you could skate all the way across L.A. uninterrupted. Some skaters made that journey and got sucked into the environment, becoming a statue or a landmark that no longer felt pain. The city is a vortex of complexity that only God could keep straight in his mind.

At least my memory is always there and even as my life falls apart in front of me I have a clear picture of the past and how blessed I was to be in a spot to know the Inglewood Skate Rats. Skateboarding was my first lady and I'm extremely loyal to her. Through thick and thin, better or worse gear- almost accepting a vow of poverty to continue doing it. So many times I hear a creeping voice urging me to skate and I get super anxious 'til I go. I know over the years I've missed out on school and seeing my family because of it- it's an addiction. There are wrinkle marks all over my face from years of exposure under our beautiful star and I am a honkey that's practically brown. My knees wobble from being blown out too many times and I have a trick elbow and wrecked shins. It feels like I've pushed thousands of miles or more over the years to skate spots or the store, or away from a bad situation.

When I think back to skating in Inglewood as a kid I hear lawnmowers and airplanes in the distance, and remember dodging cars and skating the curb cuts in every driveway on the block. Near my house were the highest curbs and some of them were painted red and I can still see Chris Elder frontside slappy grinding them at full speed, crawling up the curb with pure pressure, his trucks at a slant throwing paint chips everywhere with the glowing water of sprinklers making the background hazy as the sun set.

Made in the USA
Coppell, TX
05 May 2021